Jewelry of Ideas
The Susan Grant Lewin Collection

Ursula Ilse-Neuman

COOPER
HEWITT

This book is published in conjunction with the exhibition *Jewelry of Ideas: Gifts from the Susan Grant Lewin Collection* at Cooper Hewitt, Smithsonian Design Museum, November 17, 2017–May 28, 2018.

Jewelry of Ideas: The Susan Grant Lewin Collection is made possible in part by the Rotasa Fund, Society of North American Goldsmiths (SNAG), Gallery Loupe, Sienna Patti, William P. Short III, in memory of Nancy Jean Fulop Short, Helen W. Drutt English, Kim and Al Eiber, and Ornamentum Gallery.

This publication is made possible in part by the museum's Andrew W. Mellon Foundation Publications Fund.

Published by Cooper Hewitt,
Smithsonian Design Museum
2 East 91st Street
New York, NY 10128
USA
cooperhewitt.org

Distribution (United States) by ARTBOOK | D.A.P.
75 Broad Street, Ste. 630
New York, NY 10004
USA
artbook.com

Distribution (Worldwide x-US) by Arnoldsche Art Publishers
Olgastrasse 137
70180 Stuttgart
Germany
arnoldsche.com

Library of Congress Cataloging-in-Publication Data on record

ISBN 978-1-942303-18-3 (US)

The Deutsche Nationalbibliothek lists this publication in the Deutsche Nationalbibliografie; detailed bibliographic data are available on the Internet at www.dnb.de.

ISBN 978-3-89790-512-2 (Arnoldsche)

Director of Cross-Platform Publishing: Pamela Horn
Cross-Platform Publishing Associate: Matthew Kennedy
Color: Embassy Graphics
Printer: Printplus
Book Design: With Projects Inc.

Font: Tiempos Headline; Union Headline
2016 2017 2018 2019 / 10 9 8 7 6 5 4 3 2 1
Printed in China

Front cover image: Helen Britton (Australian, b. 1966) Coldstar Necklace from the *Dekorationswut* Series (Australia), 2012; Silver, molded plastic, paint; 41 × 18 × 0.9 cm (16 1/8 × 7 1/16 × 3/8 in.); Promised gift

COOPER HEWITT

Smithsonian Design Museum

arnoldsche ART PUBLISHERS

Contents

Foreword
By Caroline Baumann

Jewelry is more than adornment. It is a form of communication that continually advances in significance and expressivity through the design of new structures, materials, and techniques. Cooper Hewitt's collection contains many exceptional examples that reflect the variety and breadth of jewelry design: these range from an ancient Egyptian ceramic and stone beaded necklace to a pair of Victorian-era gold earrings with delicately woven inserts of human hair to an assortment of brightly colored, modern plastic jewelry. *Jewelry of Ideas: The Susan Grant Lewin Collection* celebrates the gift to Cooper Hewitt of a selection of 150 brooches, necklaces, bracelets, and rings drawn from the contemporary jewelry collection of this renowned collector. The pieces chosen broaden the international scope of Cooper Hewitt's jewelry holdings and bring important innovators into the collection. We are all grateful to Susan Grant Lewin for her extraordinary generosity, which has transformed the jewelry collection and will forever enrich the stories we are able to share.

This book, published to accompany the eponymous exhibition, illustrates a dramatic revolution in jewelry design that began in the mid-twentieth century and is represented in the Susan Grant Lewin Collection. Many thanks to With Projects for their dynamic and striking design of both the book and the exhibition. The designers of the pioneering works featured—many of whom have shared their thoughts on the design process for this publication—have shown how jewelry can function as a rich narrative, a political statement, or a discourse on identity. They have surprised us through the use of unconventional materials, such as machine parts and newspaper clippings, and subverted our expectations for the feel and appearance of classic metals and precious stones. Together, this diverse collection demonstrates jewelry's dynamic power to engage the body, the eye, and the mind.

Sincere thanks as well to Ursula Ilse-Neuman for her illuminating research and writing and for guiding us throughout the publication and exhibition process.

Collector's Statement By Susan Grant Lewin

Art, architecture, and design have always been my passion; first as a journalist (Fairchild publications, then Hearst magazines), later as creative director of a major corporation, and then, as founder of my own art and architecture public relations company.

It was by chance that my professional interests led me to become a contemporary jewelry collector. While still working as a journalist, I traveled frequently to Denmark to write about furniture. It was in Copenhagen that I fell in love with the work of Vivianna Torun Bülow-Hübe. That was the beginning!

As the creative director at Formica Corporation, I was determined to bring "culture" to the commercial manufacturer with an arts program which included lecture series, museum exhibitions, scholarships for design students, etc. As part of the program, I organized a design competition with t he goal to suggest innovative uses for a new material. Titled "Surface and Ornament," the *New York Times* called the resulting exhibition "the benchmark of design competitions."

One of the most celebrated pieces I commissioned while at Formica was Frank Gehry's Fish in ColorCore. That work was included in Gehry's 1986 retrospective at the Walker Arts Center in Minneapolis. I worked closely with design curator Mickey Friedman, who always admired my jewelry. She ended up inviting me to buy jewelry for the Walker. This gave me the opportunity to travel across the United States and visit the most important contemporary jewelers' studios—and, in the process, build my own collection.

I became an avid student of art jewelry, first of the studio craft movement after World War II and later of the current international scene. I then commissioned several leading art jewelers to participate in a traveling exhibition that stopped at the Edinburgh Festival, among other venues. As a result, several works from the exhibition are now in the permanent collection of The Art Institute of Chicago.

I became a major proponent of contemporary American jewelry, which was not as well regarded as its European counterpart at the time. In order to champion American jewelers, I wrote a comprehensive book on the subject, *One of a Kind: American Art Jewelry Today* (Harry N. Abrams, 1994).

Over the next few decades, I assembled a seminal collection of contemporary art jewelry. My collecting was driven by experimentation. I sought out works that were not about wealth or sentiment; they were about ideas and concepts—art in jewelry format. Jewelry is a piece of art that one can wear, it goes everywhere with you. The jewelry in the collection is often abstract or non-objective and includes jewelers whose work advanced the field. I built a collection with a pantheon of jewelers, representative of the absolute best artists working in jewelry across the world.

I have donated 150 pieces from my collection to the Cooper Hewitt, Smithsonian Design Museum in order to further the recognition of these groundbreaking works. I feel I am acting as a conduit for these pieces. This work will now be available to a wider audience and expertly preserved for future audiences.

Collecting and Wearing

By its nature, jewelry is the art of the personal made public. By wearing her art on her sleeve, Susan Grant Lewin aligned herself with the messages, symbolic or literal, that inform each piece in her collection. This intimate connectedness between object and wearer is unique to art jewelry, and wearing such creations frequently becomes a defiant act that identifies the wearer with concepts and propositions that are complex and unruly. The delight in wearing these creations, however, has been but one of Lewin's motivations—her pleasure in collecting contemporary jewelry also stems from her passion for supporting, and indeed shaping, this evolving field through personal relationships with jewelers and designers from across the globe.

Assembled over many decades, the Susan Grant Lewin Collection captures the diversity of contemporary art jewelry with 150 works by jewelers from seventeen countries spread across five continents, a reflection of the rapid globalization of interest in the field in recent years. While more than sixty percent of the objects were made in the last fifteen years, works by seminal American and European jewelers and designers, many of whom are still working today and continuing to influence the field, add further significance to the collection.

Art jewelry is unconventional in appearance, and in viewing it one often has to set aside questions such as how pleasing a brooch or necklace looks or whether it flatters the wearer. Instead, contemporary jewelry designers challenge us to consider the ideas and messages encapsulated in their objects, to enter into a dialogue with them and embrace their "pluralism" or openness to a wide range of aesthetic, intellectual, and emotional expressions. Breaking conventional molds to accept jewelry that crosses into the realm of sculpture or even performance art as an ongoing part of the discourse, provoking viewers to reflect on their own pre-dilections and prejudices and to consider whether they dare align themselves with the concepts being presented.
—UIN

Born of Ideas
The Susan Grant Lewin Collection
By Ursula Ilse-Neuman

(Fig. 1)

The motivation to wear jewelry predates recorded history, propelled along for more than a hundred thousand years by humankind's desire to communicate ideas symbolically and to adorn and protect themselves. Jewelry makers through the ages have responded to these basic impulses by harnessing the expressive potential in a great range of materials—natural and manmade, mundane and rare—and through inspiration and mastery of tools and techniques have transformed tangible matter into intimate objects imbued with cultural, aesthetic, and spiritual values.

(Fig. 2)

Toward the middle of the twentieth century, a new form of one-of-a-kind jewelry triumphed on both sides of the Atlantic and radically challenged the way in which jewelry had been conceived throughout Western history. Studio jewelry, as it became known in the United States, emerged in the 1940s as ground-breaking jewelers drew inspiration from contemporary art and culture rather than from conventional jewelry designs. This fundamental shift in thinking and making was carried to the forefront of artistic expression and public awareness in the 1950s and 60's by jewelry makers informed by the tenets of the studio craft movement. Distinguishing their creations from the luxury jewelry of the day, as well as from low-cost mass-produced jewelry, these iconoclasts realized their work from concept to completion, proclaiming their individuality, valuing the recognizable touch of the human hand, and making affordable jewelry that would appeal to an increasingly educated and sophisticated middle class. This avant-garde jewelry conferred status on its makers and wearers through the ideas that inspired it, not through the market value of its materials or its suggestions of wealth. In the words of art historian Blanche Brown, "Diamonds were the

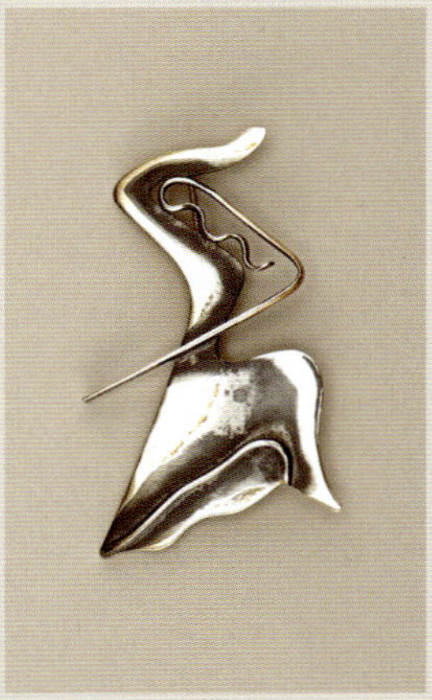

(Fig. 3)

(Fig. 4a)

badge of the philistine."[1] As can be seen in the Susan Grant Lewin Collection, jewelry's potential to convey important artistic, political, social, and personal concepts has continued to attract new generations of jewelry makers and an expanding audience for their creations.

AMERICAN PIONEERS

The origins of studio jewelry can be traced to Greenwich Village in New York City, the epicenter in the 1930s and 40's of an extraordinary community of avant-garde artists, writers, musicians, modern dancers, and filmmakers. There, inspired by the creativity around them, a group of pioneering jewelry artists set up studios in small storefront workshops and began fashioning innovative jewelry that reflected the influence of twentieth-century art movements such as Cubism, Surrealism, Constructivism, and Abstract Expressionism (Fig. 1). Largely self-trained, these radical thinkers knew little of sophisticated goldsmithing techniques but succeeded nevertheless in turning what could have been a handicap into an advantage. Sam Kramer, Art Smith, Ed Wiener, and Francisco Rabajes[2] were among the artists who were drawn to making "wearable art" through the use of simple techniques, the exchange of gold and precious stones for silver, brass, and semiprecious stones, and frequently the inspiration of modern sculpture, dance, and jazz (Figs. 2, 3, 4a,b).[3] The potential inherent in this new approach was made clear by Art Smith, one of a very few African Americans working in the field—then or since—whose extravagant neckpieces and cuffs created a new awareness of the body as a living armature. His Modernette cuff (Fig. 5) is an outstanding example of his artistry. Made of intertwined copper and brass elements, its biomorphic shape gracefully embraces the wrist, using positive and negative space in a dramatic composition that reveals patches of the wearer's skin.

(Fig. 4b)

(Fig. 5)

A turning point in the development of American studio jewelry came in 1946 when the Museum of Modern Art

(Fig. 6)

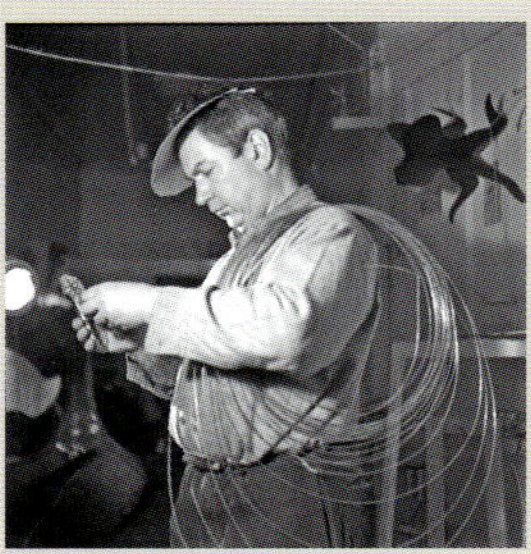

(Fig. 7)

(Fig. 8)

(Fig. 9)

(Fig. 10)

(MoMA) acknowledged jewelry as an art form in its landmark exhibition *Modern Handmade Jewelry*. The exhibition featured jewelry by renowned painters and sculptors, "artists as jewelers," along with pieces by "jewelers as artists."[4] Among the artists as jewelers were Anni Albers, whose signature *Necklace* fashioned from a drain sieve, paper clips, and a beaded chain startled viewers (Fig. 6),[5] and Alexander Calder (1898–1976), who, in particular, became an inspiration to American studio jewelers. Fabricating his jewelry with simple tools, using brass as one of his preferred materials, and often embellishing his pieces with bottle glass, ceramic shards, and wood fragments, he brought an immediacy to the jewelry-making process and demonstrated that jewelry need not depend on precious metals or high-quality stones to be of value (Fig. 7). Ed Weiner noted that in viewing Calder's wire jewelry, he "recognized a craft so specific in its limitation as to appear crude and anti-craft, yet visually very sophisticated."[6] It was a novel and challenging approach that began to appeal to a small but growing number of jewelry makers across the country.

At the same time that avant-garde jewelry was making inroads on the East Coast, a community of jewelry artists who drew inspiration from the visual arts and design was also active on the West Coast. Among the notable artists in this West Coast contingent were Margaret De Patta (1895–1964) and Claire Falkenstein, both of whom came to jewelry through the fine arts and explored sculptural qualities in works infused with light and space. Falkenstein, who was best known for her monumental sculpture, started making organically-conceived abstract jewelry in 1946, applying her metal-welding skills to enclosing space in dense cage-like or folded wire structures (Figs. 8, 9). De Patta, who had studied with Chicago Bauhaus founder Lászlό Moholy-Nagy (1895–1946), became particularly fascinated with concepts of transparency and movement in space, arguing that "problems common to sculpture and architecture are inherent in jewelry design, i.e., space, form, tension, organic struc-

(Fig. 11)

(Fig. 12)

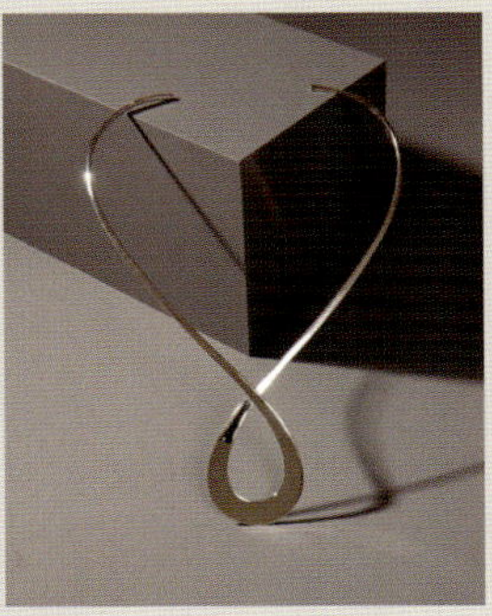
(Fig. 13)

(Fig. 14)

(Fig. 15)

ture, scale, texture, interpenetration, superimposition and economy of means. . . .”[7] The influence of De Patta's startling innovations in cutting rutilated quartz (Fig. 10) can be seen in Eleanor Moty's brooch from 1980, which expertly exploits the effects of light, space, form, and structure (Fig. 11).

While this cutting-edge experimentation was taking place in the 1950s, Scandinavian jewelry with its clarity of form and predominant use of silver was enjoying popularity in the American mainstream. Georg Jensen's jewelry captured the American market beginning with its first showing in New York in 1922, which led two years later to the opening of its flagship store on Fifth Avenue (Fig. 12).[8] Scandinavian technical precision compelled American metalworking programs such as the School for American Craftsmen (SAC) in Rochester, New York, to recruit silversmiths from Scandinavia to train their students.[9] Through this instruction a new generation of American jewelers was able to combine uncompromising technical mastery with bold American innovation. Two SAC students who mastered the dual challenges of this approach were Ronald Hayes Pearson, who allowed molten silver to suggest the fluid form for his highly polished, loop-shaped neckpiece (Fig. 13), and Swedish-born Olaf Skoogfors, who explored contrasting metal textures and striking copper and brass color combinations (Fig. 14). Balancing form, line, and color, Skoogfors's pendants frequently consist of more than one layer: a textured, cast form onto which a constructed form of metal sheet and wire is added (Fig. 15).

But Scandinavian perfection was not for everyone. After studying metalworking in Copenhagen in 1956 and 1957, and after a second sojourn in Denmark ten years later, Arline Fisch rejected the Danish approach when she discovered the jewelry of Alexander Calder and the Greenwich Village pioneers. “I needed to get away from the idea that everything had to be perfect in design and technique; that only precious metals, properly treated, constituted real jewelry, and everything had to be suitable for millions of anonymous people.”[10] Through

(Fig. 16)

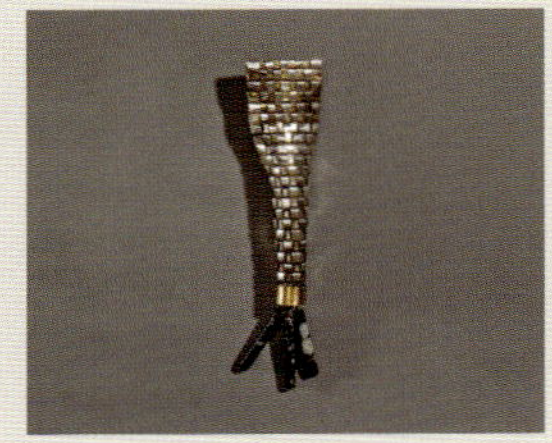
(Fig. 17)

(Fig. 18)

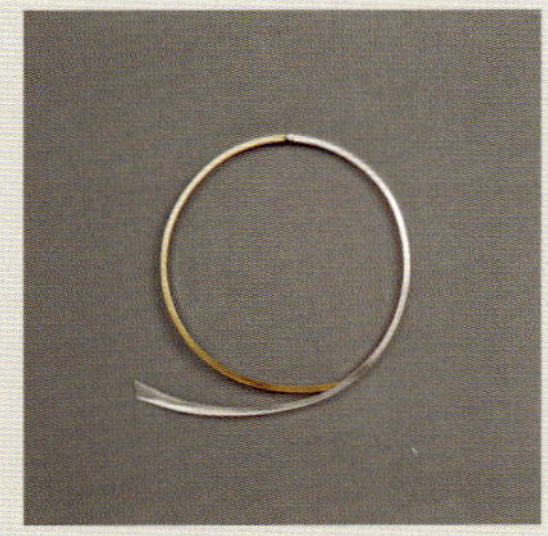
(Fig. 19)

(Fig. 20)

studying weaving, she realized the potential of combining metalsmithing skills with textile techniques to create jewelry, an insight that became all the more apparent in 1963 when she saw gold sewn into pre-Colombian textiles (Fig. 16).[11] She soon adapted a multitude of textile techniques, including weaving, twisting, knitting, knotting, and crocheting, for use with metal wire, a process that continues to occupy her to this day. Her pieces can be dense (Fig. 17) or light and airy (Fig. 18).

So, too, Betty Cooke, who remains productive in her native Baltimore, was set on her lifelong path in 1946 when she began to create handmade one-off pieces in silver that suggest a Scandinavian modernist influence in their clean, unadorned shapes and gently rounded corners, but are actually based on her training as a sculptor and her own intuitive sense of good design (Fig. 19).

In the 1960s, a new generation of American jewelry makers came of age as Andy Warhol and Pop Art burst onto the scene, displacing the modernist idioms of the 1940s and 50's and challenging views of what constituted art with transformative power comparable to that of Marcel Duchamp fifty years earlier. To make their work reflect the times, jewelry makers turned to the narrative potential of everyday objects, reconfiguring them as "readymades" and placing them in startling new contexts to take on contemporary messaging power. This became a quintessentially American form of jewelry, with content that ranged from comic to politically charged, as in the thought-provoking and pioneering jewelry statements of J. Fred Woell (1934–2015) (Fig. 20).

Two jewelers in the Lewin collection, Ramona Solberg and Robert Ebendorf, were among the first in the 1960s to assemble everyday objects into jewelry with implicit storytelling. Solberg used objects she collected during her extensive travels or ordinary items from her own household, such as the dominoes she strung on a simple leather cord (Fig. 21). Robert Ebendorf, in collaboration with then wife Ivy Ross, purposefully used throw-aways with ambiguous symbolic content.

(Fig. 21)

He made no attempt to disguise the origins of these throwaways, contending that any material, even manmade ColorCore Formica and outdated wooden clothespins, could be made into intriguing jewelry (Fig. 22). Ebendorf's references to such unglamorous activities as laundry and kitchen work introduced startling narrative content into jewelry.

EUROPEAN PIONEERS

In the 1960s, with little influence from the vigorous American studio jewelry movement, European jewelry underwent its own revolution, initiated by accomplished jewelers and impelled by social, economic, and technological changes that were transforming postwar Europe. Dutch makers were at the forefront of radical experimentation, questioning jewelry's role within a rapidly changing society through the use of new jewelry forms and materials, with German and British jewelry makers following close behind.

(Fig. 22)

Dutch Smooth

Almost unique among European countries, the Netherlands had an egalitarian society that could be traced back to the sixteenth century. Following the post-war exploitation of natural gas in the North Sea, the country enjoyed enormous prosperity, and Dutch government funding allowed jewelers greater freedom to experiment with styles, materials, and techniques that might not have had a ready market.

Two Dutch jewelers, Gijs Bakker and his wife Emmy van Leersum, led a group of artists and designers who conceived of radically new jewelry intended to reach beyond a small circle of wealthy patrons to a more youthful and less tradition-bound public (Fig. 23). Aiming to "democratize" jewelry, they made affordable, well-designed, cutting-edge works that emphasized form, function, and material.

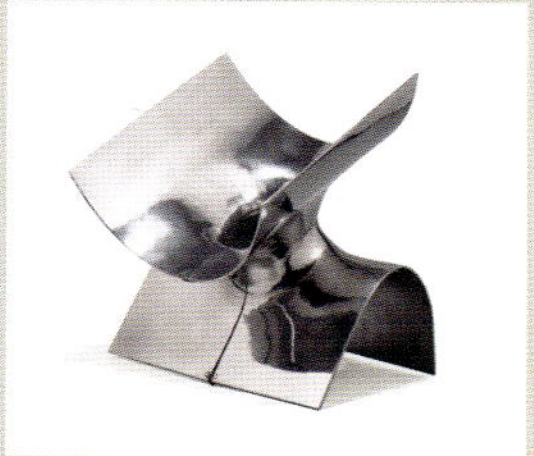

(Fig. 23)

These jewelers denounced the conventional role of jewelry and shunned all extraneous ornament, as well as the mark of the hand. They also placed a virtual taboo on gold and

(Fig. 24)

precious stones, defiantly replacing them with industrial materials such as aluminum, stainless steel, rubber, plastic, and paper. The new *Hollands Glad* (Dutch Smooth) style was eye-catching and often dramatic (Fig. 24), yet purposefully nonprecious, with designs that were well-suited for industrial production. While superficially resembling manufactured jewelry, each piece was skillfully crafted and finished to achieve the desired industrial aesthetic seen in the precise tubular shape of Van Leersum's bracelet (Fig. 25) and the elegant simplicity of the armlet by Françoise van den Bosch (Fig. 26). Such works also reflected a strong affinity with the visual arts of the time, notably the constructivist sculpture of Russian émigré Naum Gabo (1890–1977) and Swiss sculptor/architect Max Bill (1908–1994) (Fig. 27), as well as the geometric shapes of Dutch sculptor Ad Dekkers (1938–1974) (Fig. 28).

(Fig. 25)

Germany in the 1960s and 70's

After WWII, Germany was in ruins with bombed out cities and makeshift "shantytowns" housing hundreds of thousands of displaced citizens from the eastern provinces. Yet, by instituting a new currency and lifting wage and price controls in 1948, the "Wirtschaftswunder" (Economic Miracle) was launched. By 1950, industrial output tripled, and by the early 1960s, Germany was the third greatest economic power in the world.

(Fig. 26)

Democratizing jewelry was not a priority in Germany, where the apprenticeship system remained strong and skillful goldsmiths continued to feature precious materials. Even so, a number of accomplished goldsmiths defiantly violated accepted stylistic and technical practices in these materials and encouraged individuality and expressiveness as an antidote to moribund designs and standard technical perfection. The leading figure was goldsmith Hermann Jünger, who introduced an entirely new aesthetic that combined a superb painter's eye and sensitivity to three-dimensional form with consummate technical mastery. Combining the reflectivity and malleability of gold with the colors

(Fig. 27)

(Fig. 28)

and sparkle of precious stones and enamel, he translated the freedom and fluidity of his drawings into highly individualistic jewelry that clearly bore the marks of the artist's hand. Deeply committed to the wearability of his work, Jünger's jewelry never overpowered the body through gratuitous theatricality (Fig. 29). One of his distinctive boxed necklace sets (Fig. 30) contains diverse shapes ready to be strung into neckpieces on a thin gold wire. The wearer chooses the order in which the various shapes are aligned, and when the necklace is not being worn, the individual components have a separate life as an abstract composition framed by a square gray box.

(Fig. 29)

Another prominent German innovator, Friedrich Becker, was recognized for the designs of his kinetic jewelry, which is jewelry with moving components, which also appeared in the work of a few jewelers in Europe and the United States in the 1950s. Becker's technical and formal precision gained him a special place in the history of art jewelry, not only in Germany but worldwide. His carefully calibrated rotating elements affect transparency and reflectivity as a result of the body's movement and different lighting conditions. An excellent example is his silver and acrylic ring, which rotates on its axis in concert with the gestures of the wearer's hand (Fig. 31).

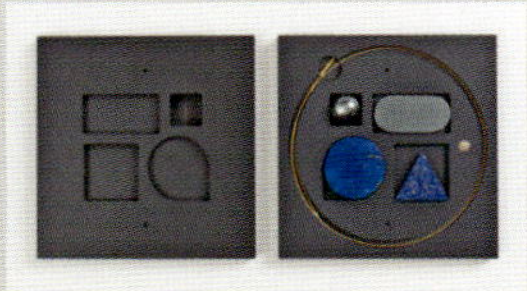

(Fig. 30)

Great Britain in the 1960s and 70's

Britain's development in the decades following World War II mirrored Holland's in the sense that British youth became an important economic and social force in the 1960s. This reality was vividly expressed by British sub-cultures such as the Teddy Boys and Mods, whose theatricality, flamboyance, and rebellious attire clashed with the norms of the middle class and captivated young people across Europe and in the United States. The following decade, yet another youth sub-culture, Britain's Punks, introduced body art, tattooing, piercing, and ripped clothes, and British designers who traded high style for street style became recognized leaders in international fashion.[12]

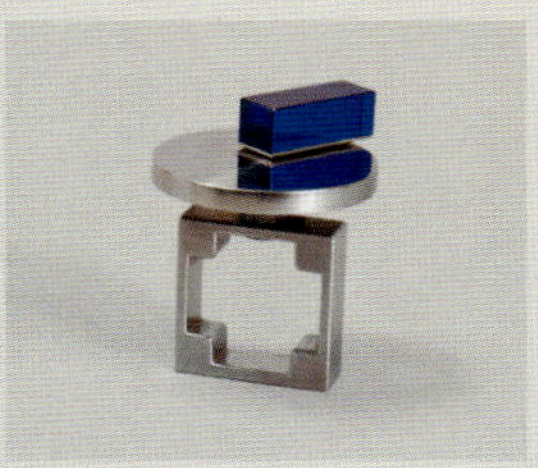

(Fig. 31)

(Fig. 32)

(Fig. 33)

(Fig. 34)

(Fig. 35)

With less governmental support than their Dutch counterparts, British jewelers had to be more aware of current fashions and commercial realities in order to seek out opportunities to show and sell their work. The leading jewelers in this youth-oriented culture were husband and wife David Watkins and Wendy Ramshaw, who, beginning in 1964, designed black and white patterned acrylic pieces with the intention of making fashion jewelry based on Op Art painting, which was enjoying popularity at the time.[13]

Watkins also included ideas from his large-scale sculptures in his jewelry, as can be seen in the clear, reductivist forms of his lathe-turned aluminum and silver *Gyro Bangle*, which expands spherically into three dimensions when worn (Fig. 32).

One of Wendy Ramshaw's signature pieces, a ring set mounted on a specially designed lathe-spun wood stand, was designed to be showcased when it was not being worn (Fig. 33). In her *Three-Cone* necklace, part of her Wedgwood Jasperware series, she experimented with delicately shaped ceramic forms that hang off-kilter on a gold wire (Fig. 34). Both Ramshaw and Watkins opened new directions for jewelry making through the unique, strongly design-oriented character of their work.

Scandinavian Jewelry

As noted earlier, Scandinavian design maintained its allure in the mainstream in Europe and America even as avant-garde jewelry widened its audience. The pioneering Swedish silversmith Vivianna Torun Bülow-Hübe, who had started making jewelry in the 1940s, was at odds with the dressy, showy school of jewelry.[14] In the 1960s she acquired an international reputation for her use of silver to create fluid curving forms in "anti-status" jewelry that was not designed to appeal solely to the wealthy. The softly rounded shapes of her elegant modernist jewelry were often embellished with glass or semiprecious stones (Fig. 35).[15]

(Fig. 36)

AN EMERGING GLOBAL INTERACTION

American jewelry and European jewelry were worlds apart before European artists began crossing the Atlantic in the 1970s to introduce their startling new work to students and faculty in American jewelry programs, only to find that they themselves were also being influenced by what they saw through the interaction.[16] Through these invigorating exchanges, what had been divergent paths on either side of the Atlantic began to coalesce and eventually reach critical mass, fueled first by greater mobility through lower-cost travel and then by the explosive growth of the Internet and social media. Museum exhibitions and new galleries featuring avant-garde jewelry, as well as expanded art school programs that encouraged students internationally to experiment with new materials and techniques, all contributed to the growth of global interest in contemporary jewelry.[17]

Despite the rapidity with which global interchange took place, contemporary art jewelry is far from standardized, as is evidenced by the diversity of the works in the Lewin collection that resist rigid categorization. Nevertheless, insight into the breadth and range of the field can be gained by considering a simple taxonomy of two broad groups: works that are primarily content driven and works that are abstract or non-objective. These very basic divisions actually serve to amplify the enormous variety and creative richness that continues to grow as new cultural influences are coupled with advances in materials and technologies.

Content-Driven Jewelry

Jewelers whose work is content driven frequently choose specific themes to which they return time after time to comment on such disparate topics as memory and remembrance, nature, the human body, and social and political ideas. Some jewelers tell their stories and convey their thoughts explicitly through found objects, symbols, and metaphors, while others prefer to use forms, materials,

(Fig. 37)

(Fig. 38)

(Fig. 39)

(Fig. 40)

(Fig. 41)

(Fig. 42)

colors, and techniques to establish metaphoric relationships that leave interpretations open to each viewer.

Storytelling Through Found Objects

Anything in existence... is continually interpreted anew, requisitioned anew, transformed and redirected to a new purpose. —Friedrich Nietzsche

Even though the inclusion of found or reclaimed objects was a new, even startling, practice when American jewelers such as Woell, Solberg, and Ebendorf introduced it in the 1960s, the approach is being used today by jewelers around the globe to create compelling objects that convey meanings, explicit or enigmatic.

Helen Britton finds rich narratives in the scrap materials she collects during wide-ranging travels from pristine beaches to grimy, industrial landscapes in her native Australia. The manmade and natural fragments she finds are given new lives in compositions that often contain allegories relating to the fragments' sources. Two of these pieces, a bracelet (Fig. 36) and a ring (Fig. 37), bring out otherwise easily overlooked aspects of the materials she uses to convey a sense of heritage or to suggest a specific place. Concerns with the unique histories embedded in found objects also motivate Lucy Sarneel (Fig. 38), Petra Zimmermann (Fig. 39), and Rian de Jong (Fig. 40).

Similarly, Mieke Groot's work allows us to see value in the vast array of discarded things she uses to create her jewelry. Her neckpiece *Dieg Bou Diar 1* was named for the brand of Senegalese tomato paste cans that a local craftsman/collaborator transformed into bead-like components. Combined with large lamp-worked glass beads blown in Amsterdam, it forms a surprising cultural hybrid (Fig. 41). From a different perspective, Sergey Jiventin finds wonder in tiny industrially-produced objects such as the small watch hands and jeweler's sawblades that become his building blocks for intricate brooches (Figs. 42, 43).

(Fig. 43)

Symbol and Metaphor

The aim of art is to represent not the outward appearance of things, but their inward significance. —Attributed to Aristotle

(Fig. 44)

Rather than finding stories within objects themselves, the Dutch artist Ruudt Peters creates substances out of which develop forms with strong symbolic values. Few jewelers are as profoundly involved with the mystical aspects of jewelry as Peters. The pendant from his *Lapis* series (Fig. 44) was inspired by the alchemists' search in the Middle Ages for the "philosopher's stone," a legendary material that could not only change base metals into silver and gold but be taken as a rejuvenating elixir. Peters created his stone pendant, which has the appearance of a religious censer, through an arduous process of grinding precious jade into a powder and then mixing the powder with liquid acrylic and pouring it into a mold.

(Fig. 45)

Estonian Kadri Mälk's approach is more intuitive and purposefully ambiguous as she transforms a prehistoric shark's tooth, coral, and hematite pearls into a prominent neckpiece (Fig. 45). The imagery evokes the deep past that connects us at a primal level in our collective consciousness, and as is the case with many of Mälk's works, the title of this piece, *It's Getting So Dark*, contributes an additional intriguing layer of meaning, with the viewer having to decide whether the title supports an idea, contradicts it, or intentionally adds to the mystery of the piece.

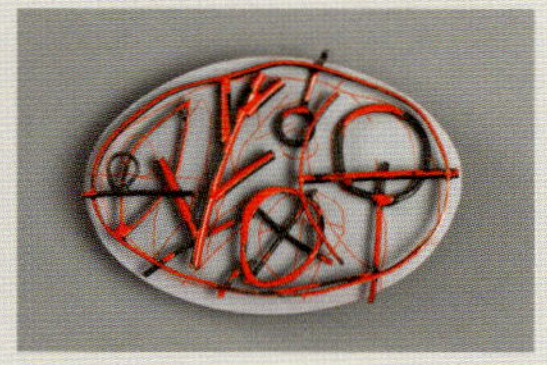
(Fig. 46)

Ramón Puig Cuyàs also holds that jewelry can communicate concepts linked to a universal sense of memory and myth and believes in the value of an artist's insights into our place in the cosmos. This brooch from his *Walled Gardens* series invites us to imagine a magical garden hidden behind the everyday fences we encounter, a metaphor for opening our senses to the many worlds around us (Fig. 46).

Hanna Hedman's series of necklaces entitled *What you tell is not always what you have experienced* (Fig. 47), reflects

(Fig. 47)

her interest in storytelling and the fact that stories can change with each telling. The long process of building her pieces involves combining metal fragments, synthetic fibers, and paint so that the final object has a life of its own within which viewers are encouraged to find their own stories.

Memory and Remembrance

Every act of perception is to some degree an act of creation, and every act of memory is to some degree an act of imagination.
— Gerald M. Edelman and Giulio Tononi

(Fig. 48)

The desire to memorialize and mourn a person through wearing portrait jewelry reached its peak in Victorian England and Civil War America with the advent of photography in the nineteenth century. In her untitled brooch (Fig. 48), Bettina Speckner uses an old tintype portrait of a mysterious couple, taking them out of context and generating an emotional impact that is heightened by the seemingly random, but carefully calibrated overlays of precious gems. Through the power of jewelry, this history-laden portrait is transported into the existential ambiguity of the twenty-first century.

(Fig. 49)

Jantje Fleischhut's insertion of incongruous modern wind turbines into the majestic stillness of an alpine landscape (Fig. 49) creates an imaginary scene that nevertheless may seem more real to us today than the lost vistas that now exist only in faded postcards.[18] Vera Siemund chose dramatized black and white portraits of "divas" of the 1960s that emphasize the manipulations of personas at that time, perhaps opening our eyes to our own acceptance of today's more sophisticated Photoshopped images (Fig. 50); Keith Lo Bue creates a mysterious infusion of discarded objects from the past with a spectral image in a transfigured timepiece, blurring our sense of time in a surreal world he conjures (Fig. 51).

(Fig. 50)

(Fig. 51)

Jiro Kamata works not with photographs but with castoff lenses, which he believes are repositories of moments to be

(Fig. 52)

remembered in people's lives (Fig. 52). The mirrored lens of his *Spiegel* pendant creates a reflected world that shifts according to the object or person appearing in the eye of its wide-angled, mirrored lens.

(Fig. 53)

Nature

One touch of nature makes the whole world kin.
—William Shakespeare

Just as prehistoric jewelry makers used seashells, carved bones, and animal parts, to reflect humankind's intimate association with the natural world, contemporary jewelry artists delve into our complex links with nature, from its beauties and mysteries to its inexorable cycle of growth and decay.

(Fig. 54)

Daniel Kruger often takes a small segment of the existing animal or plant world as a starting point for his sensuous jewelry creations. In his necklace (Fig. 53), he captures the chaotic patterns of flowers and insects behind glass in the manner of traditional lockets or portrait cameos, while alluding at the same time to science's practice of viewing organisms under a microscope. John Iversen preserves the delicate surface of a leaf by casting it in bronze (Fig. 54). Sam Tho Duong transforms the innumerable forms of natural ginger roots, a key condiment in Vietnamese cooking, into a series of works executed in electroformed silver (Fig. 55), while David Bielander is equally inspired by garlic (Fig. 56). Bones and visceral animal parts are symbols of life and death that are part of Jennifer Trask's powerful vocabulary. In her *Whorl Pendant* she creates an amalgam of carved cow and ox bone, snake vertebrae, and found plastic objects, as well as diamond encrusted wheels that suggest elements of permanence amidst the transience of life (Fig. 57).

(Fig. 55)

(Fig. 56)

(Fig. 57)

Attai Chen is also attracted to nature's cycle from growth to decay and new beginnings as is expressed in his delicately rendered neckpiece created from discarded

(Fig. 58)

fragments of paper, one of the most ephemeral materials used in jewelry (Fig. 58).

The Human Body

The body is the instrument of our hold on the world.
—Simone de Beauvoir

The human body, which has been a central element in the visual arts cross-culturally since the beginnings of civilization, can be seen in the Lewin collection in its entirety, in recognizable fragments, or as metaphoric allusions to human identity, gender, or fragility.

(Fig. 59)

Bruno Martinazzi, a renowned sculptor and goldsmith, has developed a personal, visual language that places the human body and spirit at the center of his jewelry creations. His pieces are unmistakable in their bold renderings of specific parts of the body—eyes, lips, hands, breasts, and buttocks—and convey complex layers of meaning. His pendant *Due Respiri* is a poetic evocation of two breathing mouths whose lips are not quite touching. Made from embossed gold sheets, his jewelry recalls the formal restraint found in classical sculpture while capturing the tension and vibrant energy that connects two human beings (Fig. 59).

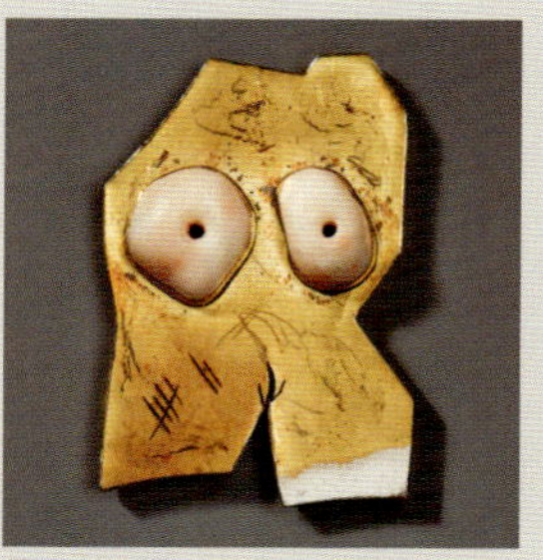

(Fig. 60)

Manfred Bischoff worked with gold, coral, and precious stones to produce intricately conceived and precisely wrought sculptural compositions in which he frequently sought to capture the moment when an idea or emotion takes on physical form. His brooch (Fig. 60) consists of a non-idealized fragment of the female body that suggests Paleolithic fertility figures such as the Venus of Willendorf.

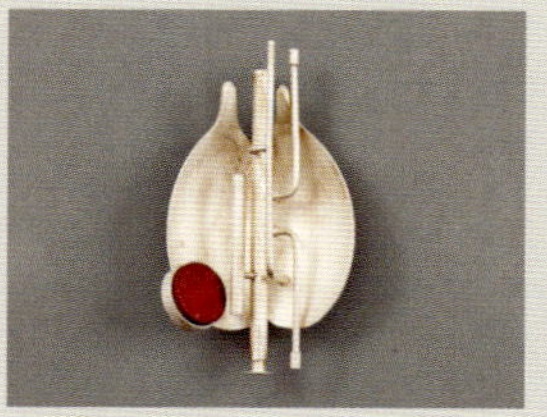

(Fig. 61)

In a more abstract, contemporary style, Katja Prins's brooch (Fig. 61) reflects her interest in the interconnectedness of human bodies and machines. In her words, "Every organic body of a living being is a kind of divine machine, or natural automaton, infinitely surpassing all artificial automatons."[19] Prins uses the blood red color and softness

(Fig. 62)

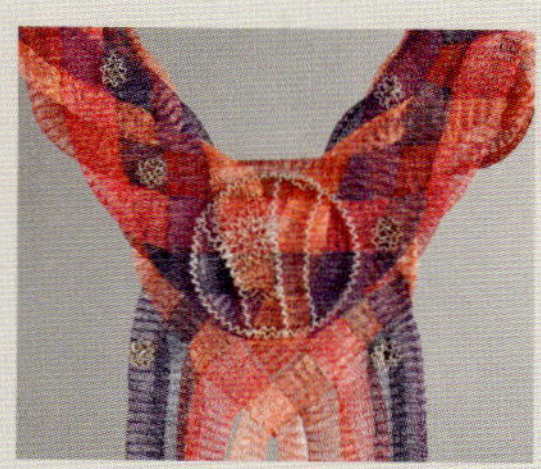

(Fig. 63)

(Fig. 64)

(Fig. 65)

(Fig. 66)

of sealing wax to contrast with the metal "skeleton" as a suitable metaphor for the vulnerability and resilience of the human body.

Doug Bucci utilizes computer-aided technologies to simulate patterns and cell forms from human biology. A diabetic, he transforms the numerical values of his own blood glucose readings into physical patterns for his necklace of glass-filled nylon, which was designed and 3D printed as an interlocking chain (Fig. 62). The underlying design consists of finely shaded light, dark, and intermittently gray cellular links that are rhythmically arranged to create an interdependent unity.[20]

Since her pioneering work in the 1960s, Arline Fisch has continued to challenge perceptions of jewelry and the body not only by changing the size of her jewelry in relation to the body but by increasingly aligning her textile-like work with body garments. Her large, flexible, knitted copper body ornament links the oftentimes mutually exclusive worlds of art jewelry and fashion (Fig. 63) and is one of her signature pieces.

Daniel Jocz explores the area where jewelry overlaps with fashion and its accessories. With a nod to Pop Art he has deposited hundreds of small rayon particles onto various silver shapes to produce colorful flocking for his playful *Candy Wear* (Figs. 64, 65, 66).

Social and Political Commentary

We [Greeks] are the only people who consider a person who takes no part in public affairs, not merely [lazy], but good for nothing. —Thucydides

American jewelers responded to the political, social, and cultural revolutions of the 1960s with works that boldly addressed the social issues of the day. The Lewin collection presents a number of more recent works with such deeply felt messages.

An inveterate story teller, African-American Joyce Scott introduces strong social undercurrents in her colorful bead-

(Fig. 67)

(Fig. 68)

(Fig. 69)

(Fig. 70)

(Fig. 71)

ed jewelry that are cartoonish yet deeply felt. Her sculptural neckpiece constructed with an off-loom weaving technique known as the peyote stitch, challenges the viewer to consider issues of gender, race, and class (Fig. 67).

Israeli jewelers Deganit Stern Schocken and Esther Knobel reflect on their country's complex history and present tensions. Schocken uses salvaged crushed aluminum cans from a security checkpoint on Israel's West Bank to convey the everyday reality of existing in a nation that must be constantly vigilant (Fig. 68). Esther Knobel's animated figures from her Immigrant series takes a lighter look at the many ways people have come to live in Israel. An immigrant from Poland, she emphasizes the blend of influences by taking metal scraps, including a colorful image from a Chinese tea box, to create a view of how Genghis Khan might have entered on a chariot (Fig. 69).

Gijs Bakker's *Blinker* brooch, part of his *Sportfiguren* series, satirizes the worship of athletes by transforming a newspaper image of the superstar Dutch striker Regi Blinker into jewelry. To add an exclamation point, he links the outsize celebrity to money by overlaying the soccer ball with an aquamarine gemstone (Fig. 70).

Iris Eichenberg symbolically expresses her interest in feminism and human relationships in narratives that are intended to leave much to the imagination. With her brooches from the *Heimat* series (roughly translated as Home or Homeland), one enters a very personal world where thread and other components that are presented in a sewing box-like container, are suggestive of warmth and healing (Fig. 71). The *Weiss* brooch, (Fig. 72) whose German title refers both to the color white and the infinitive *to know*, is a poetic joining of blank, face-shaped ovals made of white leather assembled into the porcelain branch of an imaginary family tree, not of a particular family but of all of humankind. In the words of author and critic Renee Hoogland, "Eichenberg's system always revolves around

(Fig. 72)

people . . . but here, the connections, links and junctions are ostensibly unmarked by the established rules of kinship systems."[21]

(Fig. 73)

Kiff Slemmons's *Reliquary of My Own Making* necklace (Fig. 73) is a celebration of the handmade object. The photographic images of the maker's hands and tools represent a permanent record of the process of creating jewelry, a form which to Slemmons is endangered. Through the reliquary, Slemmons also memorializes all women who work with their hands for self-fulfillment and to gain self-confidence. This, her signature necklace, is an homage to those who take their work from the utilitarian level to the spiritual.

(Fig. 74)

In her *The Mind in the Hand* collection, Esther Knobel also depicts hands at work and captures the spirit that moves them. The process that Knobel invented to make this brooch involves embroidery with steel thread on a silver surface, an arduous process that is in itself a tribute to the value of dedication and skill (Fig. 74).

(Fig. 75)

Bruce Metcalf's jewelry frequently captures the human condition with all its insecurities and fears through enigmatic faceless, alien figures (Fig. 75). Taking Metcalf's carved emaciated figure, Kiff Slemmons placed it on a silver nest with coral flames (Fig. 76) as part of a project in which she "repaired" or finished the incomplete work of other jewelry artists.

Abstract (Non-Representational) Jewelry

Abstraction is real, probably more real than nature.
—Josef Albers

(Fig. 76)

The abstract or non-objective (non-figurative) jewelry in the Lewin Collection includes works based on geometric forms and proportions in classical architecture, those relating to the more mechanistic principles of engineering, and others that are more organic in nature. Another group includes painterly works whose surfaces serve as canvases to be shown on the body instead of the wall.

(Fig. 77)

(Fig. 78)

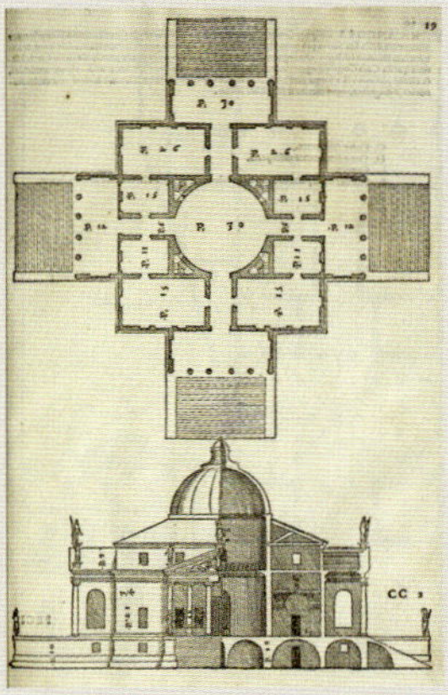

(Fig. 79)

(Fig. 80)

(Fig. 81 & 82)

The Padua School

The geometrically-inspired works of the Padua School founded by Mario Pinton (1919–2008)[22] form one of the most important components of the Lewin Collection. Pinton, a goldsmith by training, is credited with transforming the traditional goldsmith's art of Padua's nineteenth-century Istituto Pietro Salvatico through his own work and by inspiring several generations of artists to apply mastery of goldsmithing in highly creative formal compositions known for clear geometric structure without extraneous decoration. In Renaissance Italy, geometry and mathematics became the mystical as well as the practical means of achieving perfection in art. The men and women of the Padua School have adopted the classical desire for perfection and beauty in form, proportion, and material, carrying the principles further with distinctly contemporary interpretations.

Pinton's first pupil, Francesco Pavan, coupled unusual permutations of solid geometric cubes, cones, pyramids, and spheres with experimental fusions of gold, copper, silver, and nickel silver. Each Pavan piece of this period is immediately identified by the manner in which his rich chromatic patterns heighten the impact of his pure forms (Fig. 77). Renzo Pasquale similarly works with clean, architectural shapes, often overcoming technical challenges to combine such dissimilar materials as ceramic, gold, and niello (Fig. 78).

Giampaolo Babetto, the most renowned of Pinton's students, explores spatial relations and structures strongly influenced by the mathematical proportions found in Palladian buildings of the Veneto (Fig. 79). Like a composer basing variations on a few notes, Babetto often uses the cube as his starting point, only to reinvent it in highly original prismatic variations with bright pigments applied to the surfaces (Fig. 80). In two rings, combinations of parallelograms are used to create dynamic counterpoints between closed and open structures. In the 1981 ring (Fig. 81), Babetto used pure gold cut and folded into two cubes inclined at different angles,

(Fig. 83)

while in the 1995 ring (Fig. 82), he applied a coating of milky white resin to a planar surface that contrasts with the volume of the ring aperture.

The brooch by Graziano Visintin, the present director of the Padua School, maintains the school's characteristic sensitivity to the properties of gold while achieving extraordinary atmospheric effects by applying enamel and black niello to the softly shimmering gold surfaces (Fig. 83). Stefano Marchetti and Annamaria Zanella belong to the third generation of Padua jewelers who continue to build upon decades of inventive work. Marchetti uses a mosaic-like metal inlay technique in his *Map of Venice* brooch (Fig. 84), which is an imaginative abstracted representation of the shimmering waters of this fabled city.

(Fig. 84)

Zanella deliberately distanced herself from rigid geometry and unadulterated gold surfaces. She was attracted to the revolutionary ideas expressed by *Arte Povera* (literally "poor art"), a movement that took place throughout Italy in the late 1960s and 70's that employed unconventional materials and styles as a criticism of contemporary cultural and societal values. Zanella's pieces often feature gold alongside poor or humble materials including corroded iron, chipped glass, and plastic, the contrasting colors and textures of which she exploits to bring out their innate beauty.

(Fig. 85)

The surface of her brooch (Fig. 85) consists of bright yet velvety shades of gold disrupted by passages of black and red lacquer in graceful, ribbon-like effects. The astonishingly soft folds and hues Zanella achieves are the result of an extensive series of experimental firings and chemical applications that go far beyond established goldsmithing traditions (Fig. 86).[23]

(Fig. 86)

In contrast to the Padua School's preference for gold, a number of European jewelers use predominantly industrial materials in an abstract reductivist style. The selection of the appropriate metal for the rigorous constructivist approach these artists undertake is critical, and it is not surprising that engineering studies often preceded their work in jewelry.

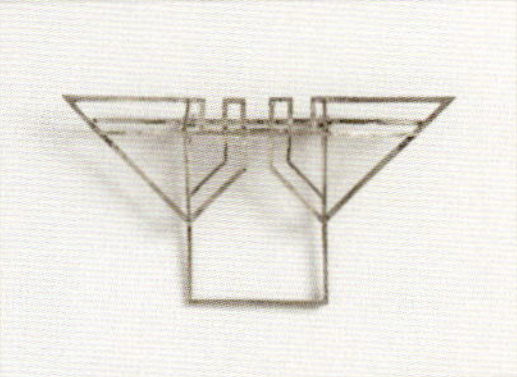

(Fig. 87)

(Fig. 88)

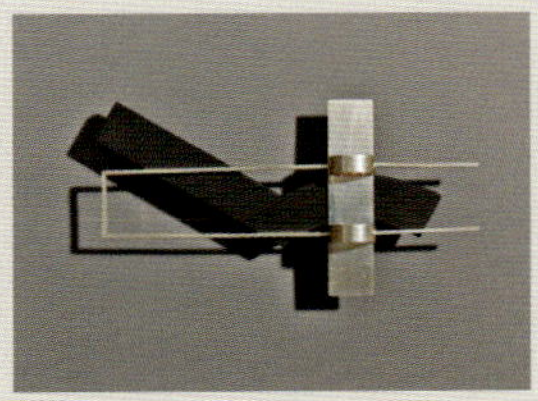

(Fig. 89)

(Fig. 90)

(Fig. 91)

Anton Cepka achieved international recognition despite having lived behind the Iron Curtain for several decades. His delicately worked jewelry, primarily in silver, is known for the precision and economy of line that make his work appear almost weightless. His designs consist of thin support elements with intermittent open spaces that resemble building struts and beams, ubiquitous features of the modern, industrialized landscape. In defiance of its appearance, Cepka's jewelry has been skillfully executed by hand using drilling, sawing, filing, and cutting, along with occasional touches of enamel paint (Fig. 87).

Peter Skubic works with stainless steel sheets whose light weight and strength allow him to create larger structures as well as jewelry. His brooches are engineering tours de force with individually constructed parts connected through compression and tension and the use of springs and magnets as well as fine steel "cables" for stability. The surfaces of his interlocking and overlapping planar steel components function as highly polished mirrors to reflect light brilliantly so that their materiality seems to dissolve. Amidst these mirrors, Skubic often interposes bold, colorful elements that add to the bewildering array of reflections, while slender steel antennas reach out into the surrounding space (Fig. 88). The steel mirrors reflect fragmented views of their surroundings in reverse, creating the shimmering unreality Skubic envisioned as the jewelry moves with the wearer.

Eva Eisler is an architect, jeweler, and designer who employs industrial materials and engineering principles to create small constructs that are inspired by the urban landscape. In a series of brooches from the 1990s, she experimented with a variety of metals held together by tension, contrasting their flexibility with the brittleness of slate (Fig. 89). In later works, she joined stainless steel flat springs, a metal component from outside of the jewelry world, into a classic "paper chain" neckpiece that is both hi-tech and eye-catching (Fig. 90).

(Fig. 92)

(Fig. 93)

(Fig. 94)

(Fig. 95)

(Fig. 96)

Organic or Biomorphic Abstractions

Abstract works also include sculptural forms that are sensitive to proportion and scale but without rigid geometrical underpinnings, subtly responding to the symbiosis between the object and the body. Organically conceived, simple, biomorphic shapes are central to Dorothea Prühl's neckpiece carved out of six pieces of elm wood left in their natural state (Fig. 91).

In contrast to the narrative nature of Bruce Metcalf's earlier work (Fig. 76), the focus of his more recent work is on sensuous, abstracted forms of fruits, flowers, and decorative shapes that make quite unmistakable references to sexuality (Fig. 92). Each wooden element is skillfully carved and painted by hand, and the composition consciously embraces the voluptuous and theatrical, recalling the exuberance of the Baroque with a contemporary frankness and vitality.

Three Japanese jewelers, Kazumi Nagano, Ritsuko Ogura, and Kyoko Fukuchi use organic abstraction in pieces that are markedly different in concept, material, and technique. They do, however, consider surface tactility, either smooth or porous, to be an important aspect of their work, an aesthetic that characterizes much of art jewelry design in Japan.

Nagano transfers the colorful two-dimensional surfaces of Nihonga, a traditional Japanese painting style she studied, into a three-dimensional origami-like shape (Fig. 93). Ogura uses disposable packing cardboard from which she carefully cuts cross-sections to enliven the textures, emphasizing that the appeal of her bracelet and brooch stems solely from her manipulations of this humble material (Fig. 94). Kyoko Fukuchi covers the carved wooden core of her brooch (Fig. 95) with hemp and multiple layers of red Urushi lacquer to accentuate the contours of its amoeba-like shape.

Svenja John's works convey a sense of organic growth despite being designed on a computer and manually assembled from individual sections of colored polycarbonate, an amorphous plastic (Fig. 96). Rather than seeking out organic shapes, Gaetano Pesce explores the potential of polyure-

(Fig. 97)

(Fig. 98)

(Fig. 99)

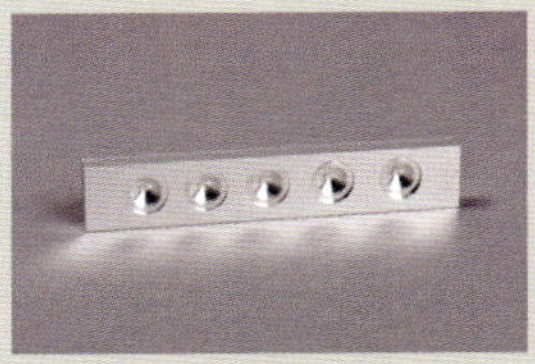
(Fig. 100)

(Fig. 101)

thane resin in wild explosions of color, with the material itself determining the final shape (Fig. 97).

Painterly Approaches

Artists who emphasize painterly surface effects use brooches as small, wearable "canvases," experimenting with a great variety of aesthetic solutions, materials, and techniques.

For more than five decades, Thomas Gentille has resolutely explored concepts, materials, and techniques that combine a painter's eye for line, color, and light with an architect's knowledge of proportion and form.[24] At the center of Gentille's art are the chosen materials he cuts, slices, and deconstructs to uncover their unique properties. He creates visually and texturally sophisticated surface compositions with intricate balances that may be purely geometric or organically rhythmic. Although he occasionally uses gold for its unsurpassed light collecting and reflecting qualities, he focuses primarily on alternative materials that have little or no traditional association with jewelry. His brooches use wood laminates, pigmented brimstone and bronze (Fig. 98) enlivened with gold flakes (Fig. 99), pure aluminum (Fig. 100), and the intricately executed eggshell inlay brooches, which have become his signature works (Fig. 101).

Jamie Bennett works exclusively with opaque enamel, avoiding illusionary space to focus purely on the surface relationships of color and pattern, creating frameless paintings through his innovative enameling process. In his *Priori* series in the late 1980s, Bennett replaced the traditional metal supports with an electroformed copper base on which he applied his refined designs with tiny brushstrokes. The later series, represented by his *Postpriori II* brooch (Fig. 102), returns to the frontal, two-dimensional approach, celebrating the decorative nature of jewelry with influences from both western and non-western historical motifs. Unlike the majority of contemporary jewelry makers, Bennett accepts his work as decorative and jewelry's function as ornament.

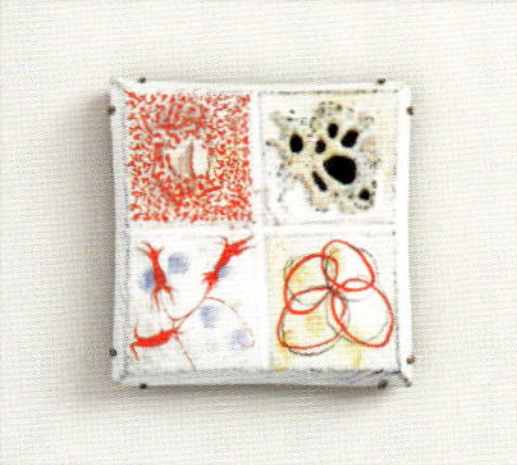

(Fig. 102)

Karen Pontoppidan is another jeweler who adopts a painter's approach. In her *Canvas 49* (Fig. 103), Pontoppidan wrapped and folded a painted canvas over geometrically-shaped wood, transforming the "painting" into three dimensions. She then embellished the surface with appliquéd jewelry medallions, thereby underscoring the interrelatedness of jewelry and the fine arts and voicing her opinion in an ongoing art jewelry discourse.

Subverting Conventions

The artist becomes a manipulator of signs more than a producer of art objects, and the viewer (becomes) an active reader of messages rather than a passive contemplator of the aesthetic or consumer of the spectacular. —Hal Foster

(Fig. 103)

Conceptual jewelry artists emphasize the intellectual idea embedded in jewelry and the social and cultural contexts in which jewelry functions. These artists question and subvert jewelry's conventions and value systems and reveal the human foibles that have long attended the desire to own these recognized symbols of wealth, status, and cultural identity.

Otto Künzli, an accomplished goldsmith, writer, and mentor, is arguably the most internationally influential jewelry artist, exposing the social, political, and cultural issues surrounding jewelry in provocative and masterfully executed designs that often display a barbed sense of humor. A Künzli piece that has become a widely recognized icon is his 1980 *Gold Macht Blind* (Gold Makes You Blind) bracelet (Fig. 104), in which a gold ball is completely shrouded in a featureless black rubber tube, metaphorically returning gold to the darkness of its origins. Delving deep into jewelry's past, and its many roles over time, he criticizes the myth of the precious, yet admits nevertheless the power of gold's allure, even when it is invisible, testing its wearer's faith in the integrity of the artist.

(Fig. 104)

In his 1986 neckpiece, one of a series, Künzli suspended an ornate picture frame fragment on a fine steel cable.

(Fig. 105)

(Fig. 106)

(Fig. 107)

(Fig. 108)

By using a normally unnoticed border, generally intended only to embellish and enhance the central subject, to replace the gemstone or portrait sitter (Fig. 105) he questions the relative importance of the jewelry versus the wearer. In another piece, *Das Bild* (The Image), he simply put a clip-frame on a postcard, making the pretty image a wearable and easily exchangeable brooch. The act is not only a critical inquiry into the expectation of what adornment means today but also the use of the "brooch" as documentation of an experience or event that is conducive to discovery (Fig. 106).

When Künzli was confronted with an active anti-smoking campaign during a 1988 visit to New York, he was motivated to take a stand "against fanatical discrimination" and interested in "the performative and communicative character of smoking and with the magical and ritual aspects that it was originally associated with." Künzli's inherently subversive approach to the function of jewelry as a tool for non-conformity is expressed with tongue-in-cheek humor against governmental control over human behavior in *The Manhattan Piece* and its accompanying manual on how to use the tubular piece most effectively (Fig. 107). The user blows out the smoke, without inhaling, through a small mouthpiece into a tube that is hidden in clothing or worn as a necklace so that the smoke comes out in an entirely different place through a small aperture that can be worn in the buttonhole or as a brooch.

Künzli's gift is that while his jewelry is about jewelry, he has made his work all the more powerful through his sensitivity to the very human aspects of wearing jewelry and his ability to create objects and images equal to his ideas.

Ted Noten likes to break away from the limiting mold to which he feels art jewelry has been confined. Instead, he strives to expand his audience beyond collectors and museums as he challenges and invades our comfort zone with jarring combinations of the familiar and the incongruous, often through public performance. Two of his pieces in the

(Fig. 109)

Lewin collection feature the unusual, not to say the repulsive: *Crazy Glasses*, in which a ratty piece of fur serves as a counterweight to a pair of glasses (Fig. 108), and *Fred*, in which a fly and pearl are embedded in his signature material—cast acrylic (Fig. 109).

Noten joins in the effort to democratize jewelry, not only by shunning precious materials but also by reaching a broader audience beyond art jewelry aficionados. In order to have everyone enjoy the status of a Mercedes Benz, he cut out fragments from the car's bodywork and then offered them for sale as brooches (Fig. 110).

Conclusion

By changing the very nature and forms of jewelry and questioning jewelry's role(s) in society today, contemporary jewelers are opening new directions of discourse. Old forms are reinvented and new territories are carved out in wearable pieces that reflect the rapid pulse and confrontations of contemporary society and culture. Under the transformative power of globalization, an increasing number of jewelers are moving away from the physical object by crossing over into other fields—the virtual and the unwearable through videos and film, installations and performances.

Amidst these expanded forms of expression and the broader consideration of the philosophical, sociological, and anthropological contexts of jewelry, the fundamental reasons for jewelry's age-old attraction endure—indeed, they are written in our genes. Jewelry is inextricably and intimately linked with the body—with our identity and our affinities. As one of today's most vital expressions within the visual arts, contemporary jewelry continues to attract new devotees with works that embody complex and dynamic balances—the sophisticated and the instinctive, the intellectual and the sensual, the personal and the universal, the cool and the hot—and the message that is being proclaimed is clear—jewelry belongs to humanity.

(Fig. 110)

NOTES

1 Milton W. Brown, Blanche R. Brown, Ed Wiener, *Jewelry by Ed Wiener: A Retrospective Exhibition* (New York: Fifty/50 Gallery, 1988–1989), 13.

2 Ed Weiner and Francisco Rebajes are represented in the Cooper Hewitt collection.

3 For a full discussion of the jewelers of the American Studio Jewelry Movement see Toni Greenbaum, *Messengers of Modernism: American Studio Jewelry* (Paris and New York: Flammarion, 1996).

4 Pioneering jewelers of the 1940s who appeared in that exhibition included Sam Kramer, Harry Bertoia, Margaret De Patta, Paul Lobel, and Adda Husted-Andersen.

5 The necklace exemplifies the impact of European artists who had founded the Bauhaus and were forced to flee Nazi Germany. Prominent among these were Anni and Josef Albers, who taught at Black Mountain College in North Carolina from 1933 to 1949 (where the necklace was made with Alex Reed), László Moholy-Nagy, Marguerite Wildenhain, and Walter Gropius, founder of the Bauhaus, who moved to the United States in 1937. Individually and collectively these émigré artists introduced Bauhaus teaching concepts into their courses and introduced craft into the fuller context of art and design.

6 Brown et al, *Jewelry by Ed Wiener*, 33.

7 As quoted in Margaret De Patta, *Design Quarterly* 33 (1955), unpaginated.

8 See Susan Weber Soros, "Building an International Reputation: The Georg Jensen Phenomenon in the United States, 1915–1973," in *George Jensen Jewelry*, David A. Taylor, editor (New Haven and London: Yale University Press, 2005), 103.

9 Two notable craftsmen/teachers at the School for American Craftsmen were John Prip, a Danish-American trained in Copenhagen, and Hans Christensen, who headed Georg Jensen's model department in Denmark.

10 Arline Fisch, personal communication, 2016.

11 Interview with Arline Fisch, *Art Jewelry Forum*, https://artjewelryforum.org/arline-fisch-hanging-gardens-0

12 In 1965, Mary Quant's miniskirt appeared, and Chelsea became an international conglomerate of fashion, cosmetics, fabrics and other consumer items that helped to make London a trend-setting capital.

13 David Watkins, draft essay for the Society of Jewellery Historians, September, 2001.

14 Ilse Crawford, "Vivianna Torun Bülow-Hübe," http://maharam.com/stories/crawford_vivianna-torun-bulow-hube

15 Her jewelry was worn by noted celebrities, including Brigitte Bardot, Ingrid Bergman, and Billie Holiday.

16 Visitors included David Watkins, Wendy Ramshaw, Gijs Bakker, Emmy van Leersum, Hermann Jünger, and Claus Bury. Watkins noted the influence of Stanley Lechtzin, Olaf Skoogfors, Albert Paley, and Arline Fisch. Personal communication, September, 2001.

17 This globalization can be tracked through the changes appearing in the annual exhibition known simply as "Schmuck," the German word for jewelry, which has attracted serious jewelers, curators, and collectors to Munich, Germany, for over fifty years. In 1959, its inaugural year, 100 jewelers were invited to participate from thirteen European countries, but in 1996, 256 applications were received from twenty-eight countries, and in 2016, there were 770 submissions from thirty-six countries.

18 "A picture is a secret about a secret, the *more it tells you the less you know*," Diane Arbus; "*Photography is a reality so subtle that it becomes more real than reality,*" Alfred Stieglitz.

19 Gottfried Wilhelm Leibniz, *Monadology, §64, 1714, translated from the German by Robert Latta*, http://philosophy.eserver.org/leibniz-monadology.txt

20 Ironically, the latest medical experiments include the replacement of fine veins with artificial, computer-created ones. Deutsche Welle, "Fit und Gesund," December 26, 2016.

21 *Iris Eichenberg: Weiss*, introduction to exhibition brochure, Galerie Louise Smit, Amsterdam, 2005.

22 The Padua School denotes a specific jewelry style that originated in the Istituto Pietro Selvatico in Padua under the leadership of Mario Pinton.

23 The necklace was inspired by the luxurious early twentieth-century plissé fabrics made by Mariano Fortuny (1871–1949).

24 Excerpted from Ursula Ilse-Neuman, "Thomas Gentille's Jewelry: A Creative Continuum," in *Thomas Gentille: Twenty-First Century*, exhibition catalogue (Montclair, New Jersey: Gallery Loupe, 2010), 13–14.

Display Quote Sources

The sources for the display quotes on pages 20 through 33 are:

Friedrich Nietzsche in *On the Genealogy of Morality*, as quoted in Leo Spinks, *Friedrich Nietzsche* (London and New York: Routledge, Taylor & Francis Group, 2003), 71.

Aristotle's *Poetics*, Bekker 1451b1,5, in reference to poetry [art], which "tends to express the universal, history gives the particular."

Gerald M. Edelman and Giulio Tononi, *A Universe of Consciousness: How Matter Becomes Imagination* (New York: Basic Books, 2000), 101.

William Shakespeare, *Troilus and Cressida*, act 3, scene 3.

Simone de Beauvoir, *The Second Sex*, translated by Judith Thurman (New York: Alfred Knopf, 2009), 44.

Thucydides, *History of the Peloponnesian War*, Book 2, Chapter 40.

Josef Albers, as quoted in *Arts/Canada* 23 (1966): 46.

Hal Foster, "Subversive Signs," in *Art in Theory: 1900–1990*, ed. by Charles Harrison and Paul Wood (London: Blackwell, 1992), 1066.

Simone de Beauvoir, *The Second Sex*, translated by Judith Thurman (New York: Alfred Knopf, 2009), 44.

Supplementary Image Sources

Fig. 1: Greenwich Village artists exhibit their work, 1947; Everett Collection Historical / Alamy Stock Photo

Fig. 2: *Roc* Pendant, Sam Kramer, 1958; Sterling silver, 14k gold, ivory, horn, taxidermy eye, coral, tourmaline, garnet; cast, fabricated; 4 3/4 x 2 1/4 x 3/4 in. (12.1 x 5.7 x 1.9 cm); Object: Museum of Arts and Design, New York, purchased by the American Craft Council, 1967; Photo: John Bigelow Taylor, 2007

Fig. 3: Dancer Brooch (New York, New York, USA), 1947; Ed Wiener (American, 1918–1991); Silver; 8 x 9.8 x 0.7 cm (3 1/8 x 3 7/8 x 1/4 in.); Cooper Hewitt, Smithsonian Design Museum, Gift of Michele Wiener, 1991-169-1. Photo © Smithsonian Institution

Fig. 4a: Isamu Noguchi, *Cronos*, 1947/cast 1963, Bronze and steel wire on stone base; 85 x 24 1/8 x 26 7/8 in. (215.9 x 61.3 x 68.3 cm); artist's base: 4 5/8 x 31 1/2 x 17 3/4 in. (11.7 x 80 x 45.1 cm); Regents Collections Acquisition Program and Thomas M. Evans, Jerome L. Greene, Joseph H. Hirshhorn, and Sydney and Frances Lewis Purchase Fund, 1986; Hirshhorn Museum and Sculpture Garden, Smithsonian Institution; Photography by Lee Stalsworth

Fig. 4b: Set design for Martha Graham's *Judith*, 1950. Isamu Noguchi. © The Isamu Noguchi Foundation and Garden Museum, New York / Artist Rights Society [ARS].

Fig. 6: Necklace, Anni Albers, ca. 1940; Drain strainer and paper clips; Length: 16 in. (40.6 cm), strainer: 3 in. (7.6 cm) diameter; The Josef and Anni Albers Foundation, 1994.14.16; Photo: Tim Nighswander/Imaging4Art; © 2017 The Josef and Anni Albers Foundation / Artists Rights Society (ARS), New York

Fig. 7: © 2017 Calder Foundation, New York / Artists Rights Society (ARS), New York

Fig. 10: Pendant, Margaret De Patta, 1948; Gold, rutilated quartz; 3 1/4 x 1 1/8 x ¾ in. (82.6 x 28.5 x 19 mm), without chain; Margaret De Patta Archives, Bielawski Trust, Point Richmond, California; Photo courtesy of George Eastman House, International Museum of Photography and Film

Fig 12: Store Front Georg Jensen Inc. 667 Fifth Avenue, New York, NY, ca.1935–44; From Christian Ditlev Reventlow, Georg Jensen Solvsmedie Gennem Fyrretyve Aar, 1904–1944 (Copenhagen; Nordlunf [1944] *Courtesy of Drucker Antiques*)

Fig. 14: Brooch (USA), 1972; Olaf Skoogfors (American, b. Sweden, 1930–1975); Silver, copper, brass; 6.7 x 5 x 1.8 cm (2 5/8 x 1 15/16 x 11/16 in.); Cooper Hewitt, Smithsonian Design Museum, Gift of Edna Sloan Beron, 1991-56-1. Photo © Smithsonian Institution

Fig. 16: Ceremonial Cloak, Early Intermediate Moche, ca. 4th-8th centuries, Gold, textile, 41 x 22, Private Collection; Photo: Arline Fisch

Fig. 20: *The Good Guys* Pendant, J. Fred Woell, 1966; Walnut, steel, copper, plastic, silver, gold leaf; 4 x 1/2 in. (10.2 x 1.3 cm); Object: Museum of Arts and Design, New York, gift of the Johnson Wax Company, through the American Craft Council, 1977; Photo: John Bigelow Taylor, 2008

Figs. 23 & 24: Halskraag/Shoulder piece,1967, Gijs Bakker, *collection Stedelijk Museum's-Hertogenbosch /NL*

Fig. 26: Bracelet (The Netherlands), 1971; Francoise van den Bosch (Dutch, 1944–1977); Aluminum; 9.5 x 9.8 x 2.2 cm (3 3/4 x 3 7/8 x 7/8 in.); Cooper Hewitt Smithsonian Design Museum, Museum Purchase from the Decorative Arts Association Acquisition Fund, 1993-114-14-a, b. Photo © Smithsonian Institution

Fig. 27: Sculpture: *Endless Loop*, 1953-56; Max Bill; Bronze; H x W x D: 125 x 125 x 80 cm); © SABAM; Foto: Bart Huysmans en Michel Wuyts; Middelheimmuseum

Fig. 28: Broken Circle, Ad Dekkers, 1976; Spaarndammerdijk, Amsterdam, Netherlands; Central Government Real Estate Agency.

Fig. 33: Picasso's Ladies no. 66—Rings for Woman in an Armchair Rings on Stand (England, 1999–2000); Wendy Ramshaw (British, b. 1939); Gold, amethyst, blue topaz, emerald (rings), painted wood (stand); 18.7 x 6.9 cm (7 3/8 x 2 11/16 in.); Cooper Hewitt, Smithsonian Design Museum, Museum purchase from General Acquisitions Endowment Fund, 2001-13-1/7. Photo: Ellen McDermott © Smithsonian Institution

Fig. 75: Figure Pin #147 (Wingnut and Errant Dandelion) Two-part Brooch and Holder (Philadelphia, Pennsylvania, USA), 1997; Bruce Metcalf (American, b. 1949); Maple, electroformed copper, brass, silver, carved Plexiglas, thermoplastic (Delrin), gold leaf; 24 x 24 x 6 cm (9 7/16 x 9 7/16 x 2 3/8 in.); Cooper Hewitt, Smithsonian Design |Museum, Museum purchase from Smithsonian Institution Collections Acquisition Program and Sarah Cooper-Hewitt Funds, 1998-14-1-a/c Photo © Smithsonian Institution

Gallery of Jewelry

Art Smith

Modernette Cuff Bracelet;
Designed 1948

Pioneering Jewelers

Contemporary jewelry has its foundation in the work of the pioneers of the studio jewelry movement. These makers broke boundaries by challenging historical and cultural norms of jewelry making by incorporating influential artistic styles of the day into their work. Emerging on both sides of the Atlantic during the mid-twentieth century, these radical innovators moved away from a reliance on precious materials and established forms, and encouraged experimentation in craft and usage.

Claire Falkenstein

Necklace;
ca. 1965

Betty Cooke

Necklace,
1948

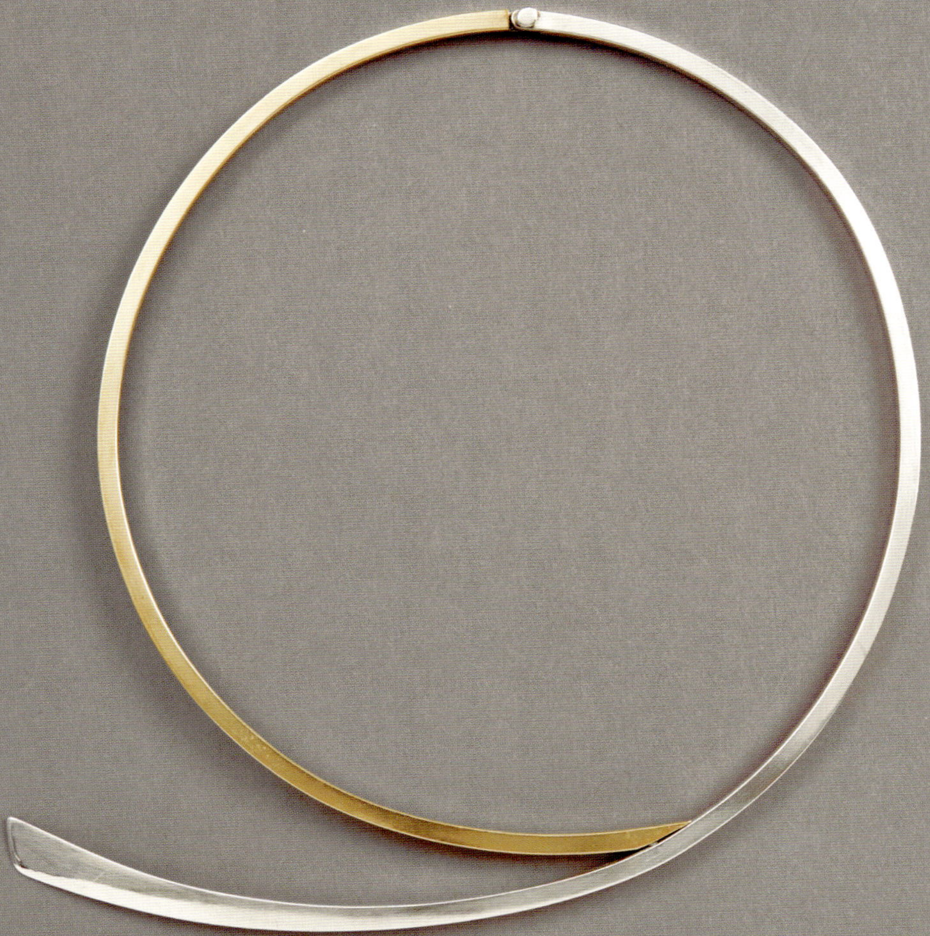

Betty Cooke
Ring; 1985

Eleanor Moty
Tourmaline Brooch II;
1980

Model No. 203A
Bangle Bracelet, 1968

Olaf Skoogfors

Necklace:
1973

Robert Ebendorf, Ivy Ross

Necklace from the ColorCore Personal Adornment Series; 1983

Ramona Solberg

Necklace;
1989

David Watkins
Gyro Bangle Bracelet;
Designed 1976
(opened, collapsed)

Emmy van Leersum

Bracelet;
ca. 1980

Hermann Jünger

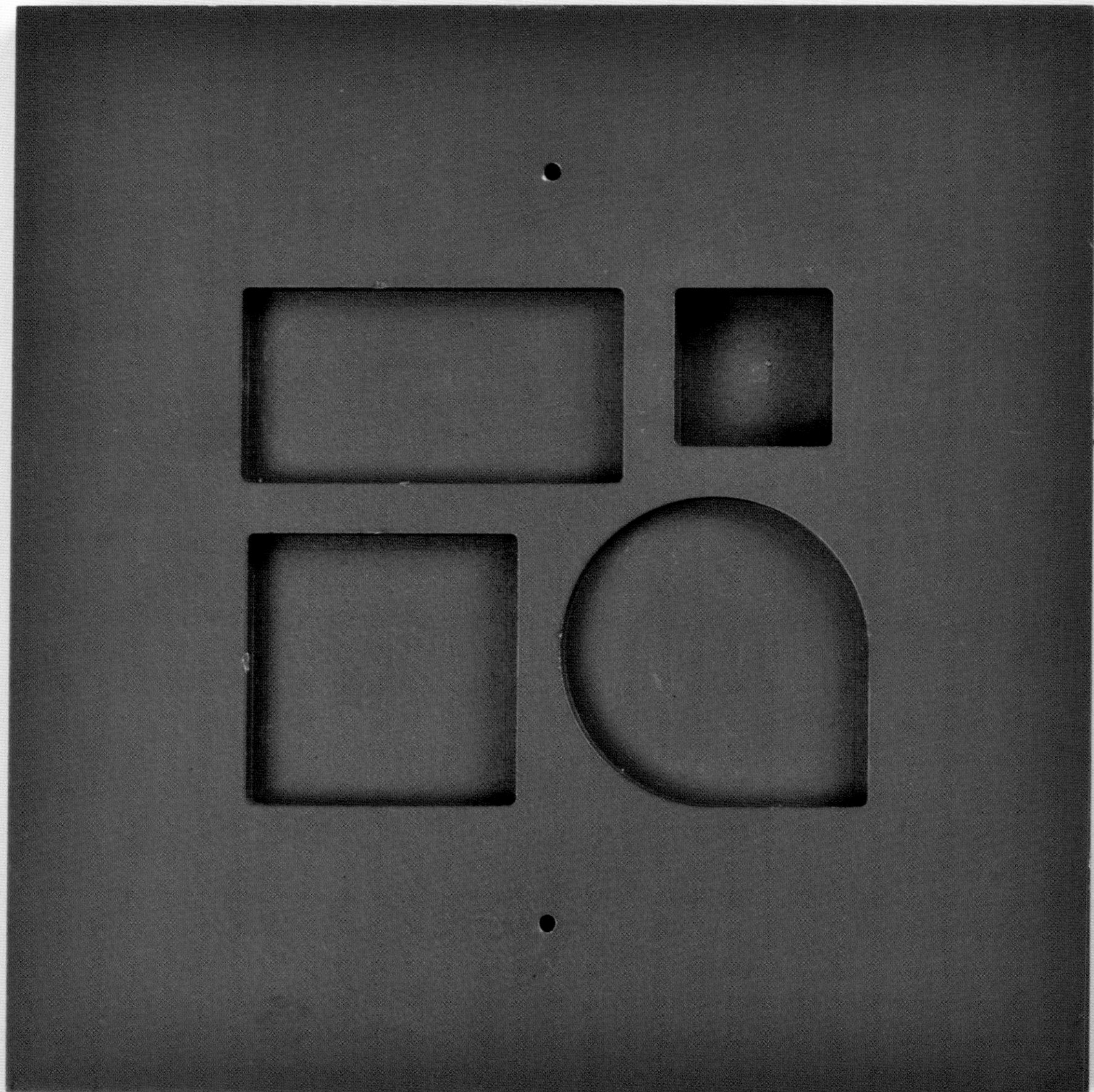

Necklace with Pendants and Box from *Serie Kasten* (the Box Series); 1993

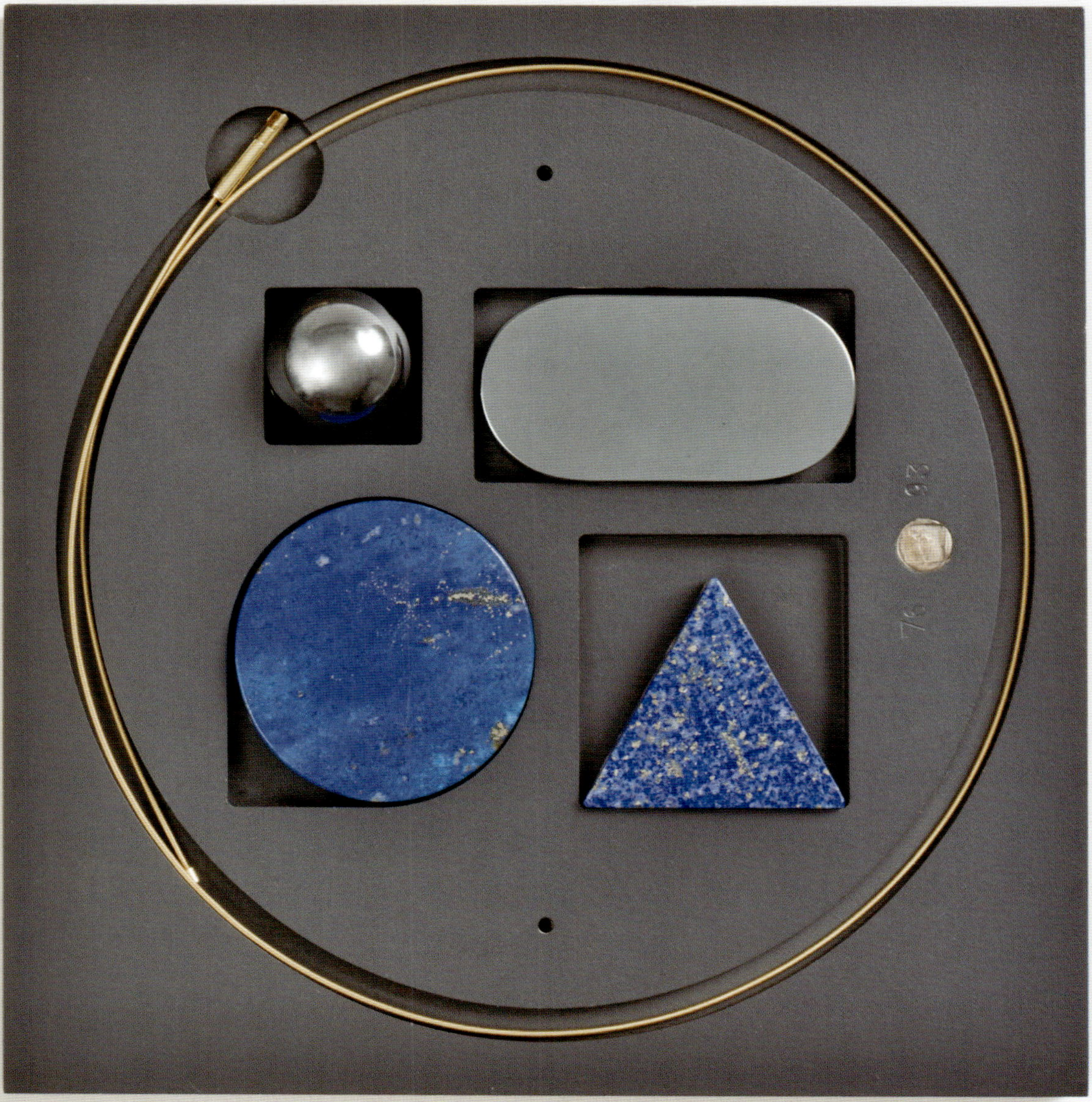

Wendy Ramshaw

Three Cone Necklace from the Wedgwood and Wendy Ramshaw Collection: 1982

Friedrich Becker

Kinetic Ring;
1993

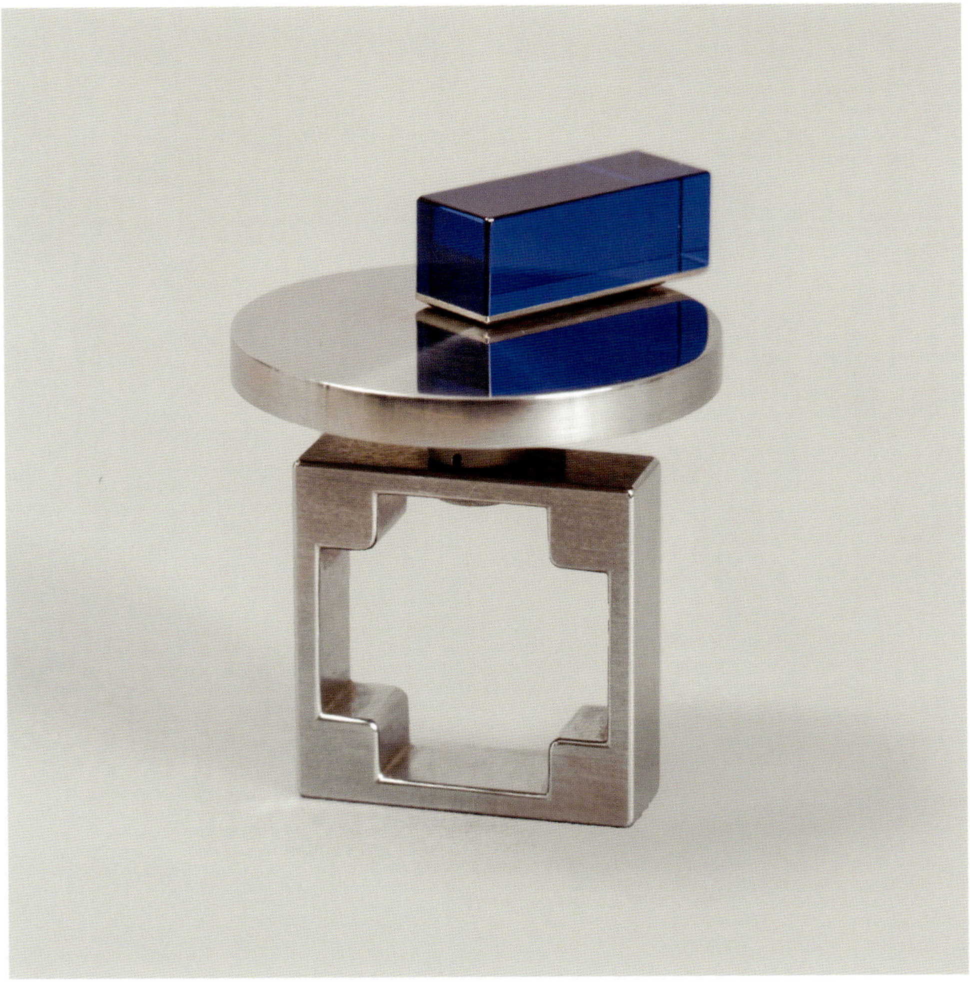

Rian de Jong

Ring from the NY NY…
right before my eyes Series;
2009

Content-Driven Jewelry

Content-driven jewelry explores and comments upon cultural and societal themes and issues. Each piece has a story to tell evoked through allegory—such as symbols and metaphor—or through the use of literal forms, like material and color. These allusions may reveal aspects of the human condition and communicate a jeweler's perception of the world. Some makers leave interpretations open, allowing wearers and viewers to create their own stories.

Helen Britton

Ring from the *Dekorationswut* Series; 2013

Helen Britton

Bracelet from the *Dekorationswut* Series; 2013

Sergey Jivetin
Knot Brooch from the Singularity Series; 2007

Sergey Jivetin
Shield #3 Brooch from the Time Structures Series; 2005

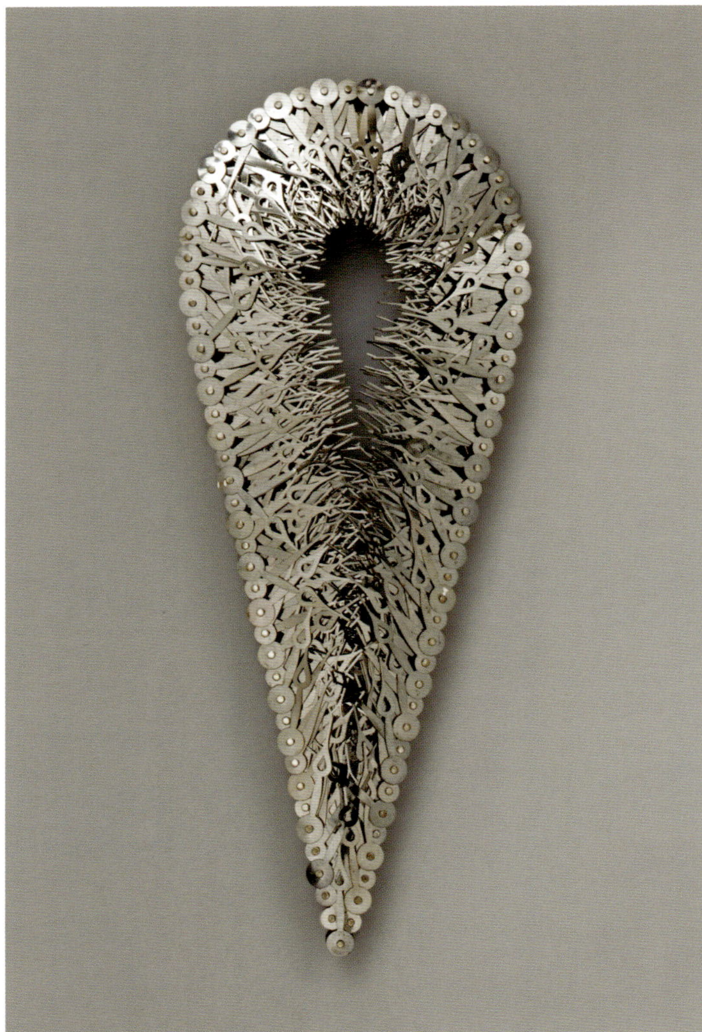

Petra Zimmermann

Brooch; 2010

Dieg Bou Diar 1 Necklace from the *Dieg Bou Diar* Series; 2006

Beppe Kessler
Pin Brooch from the Collection of different pin brooches Series; 1992

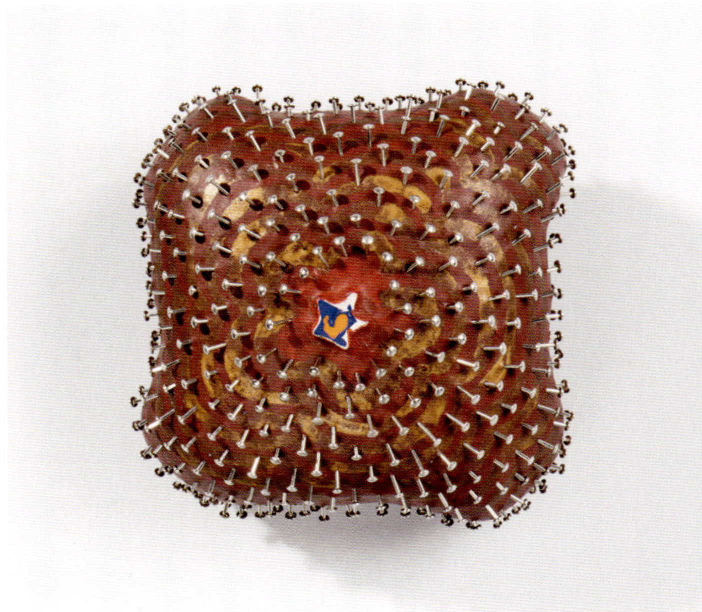

Johanna Dahm
Ring and mold from the fast ASHANTI Series; 2002

Daniel Kruger

Necklace;
1987

Brooch No. 953 from the Walled Garden Series; 2004

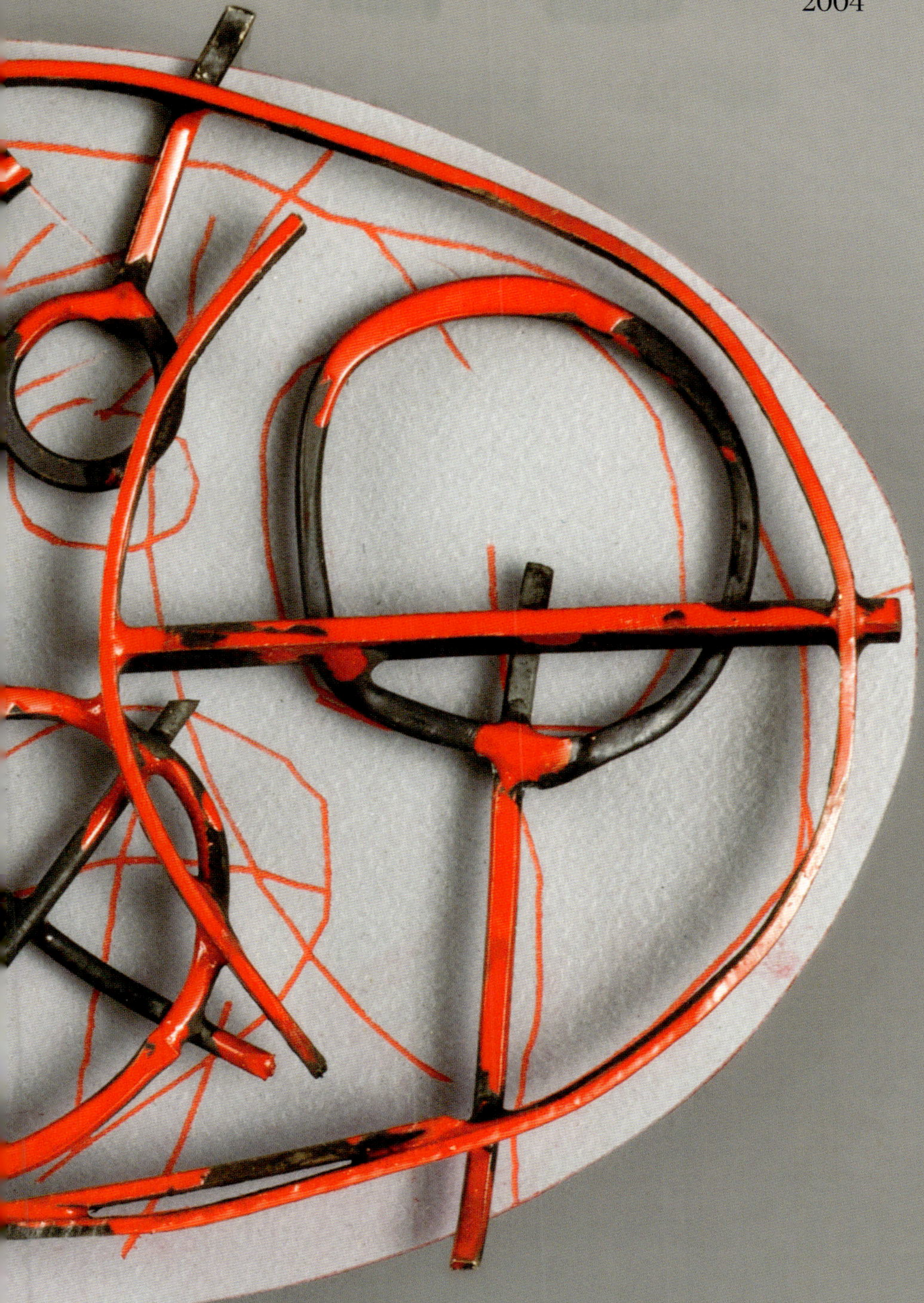

Hanna Hedman
Necklace from the
What you say is
not always what you
have experienced
Series; 2009

Kadri Mälk
It's Getting So Dark
Necklace; 2015

Ruudt Peters

Necklace from the Lapis Series; 1997

Bettina Speckner

Brooch;
2005

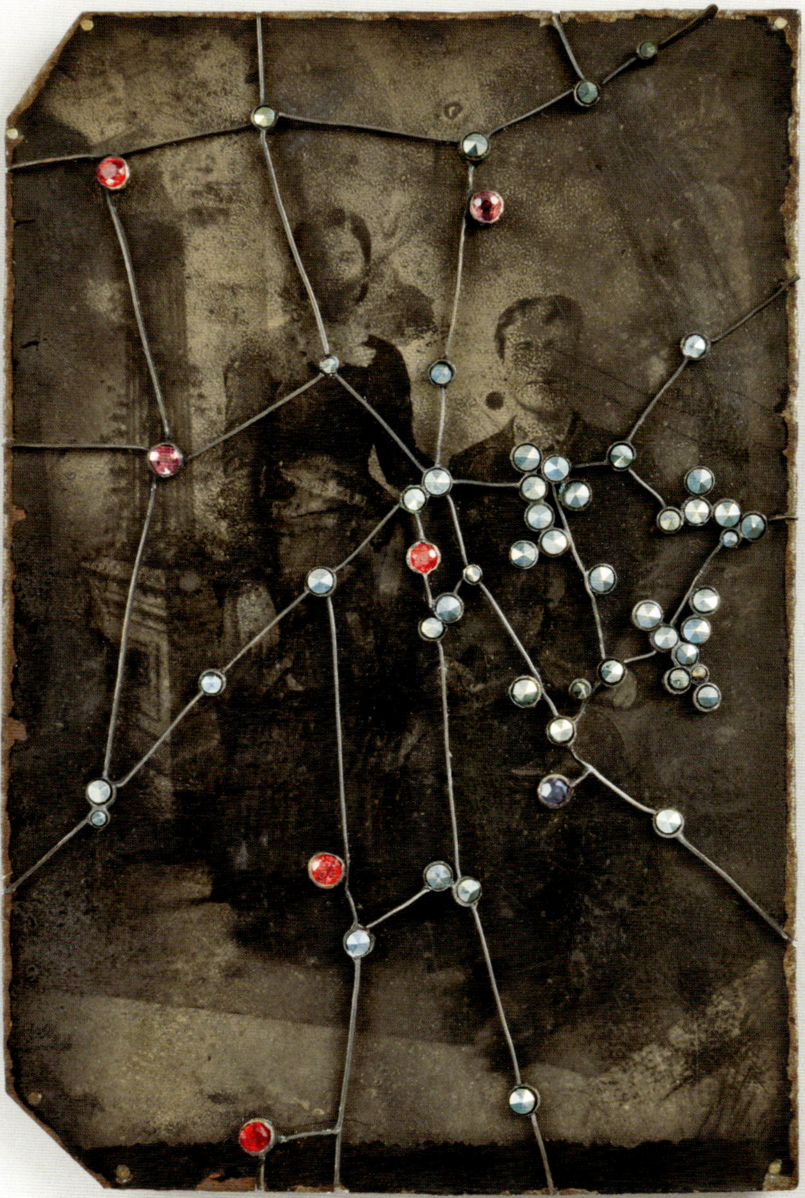

Keith Lo Bue

Untitled (15) Brooch;
1992

Jiro Kamata

Pendant Necklace from the *Spiegel* Series; 2010

Jantje Fleischhut

Be Long in Coming
Brooch from the
Dolomitensagen Series;
2008

Helen Britton

Coldstar Necklace from the *Dekorationswut Series*, 2012

David Bielander

Garlic (*Knoblauch*)
Pendant; 2009

Daniel Kruger

Necklace;
2015

Attai Chen
Untitled (5)
Necklace from the
Compounding Fractions
Series; 2010

Jennifer Trask
Whorl Pendant
from the Embodiment
Series; 2010

Sandra Enterline

Egg Pendant Necklace;
ca. 1991

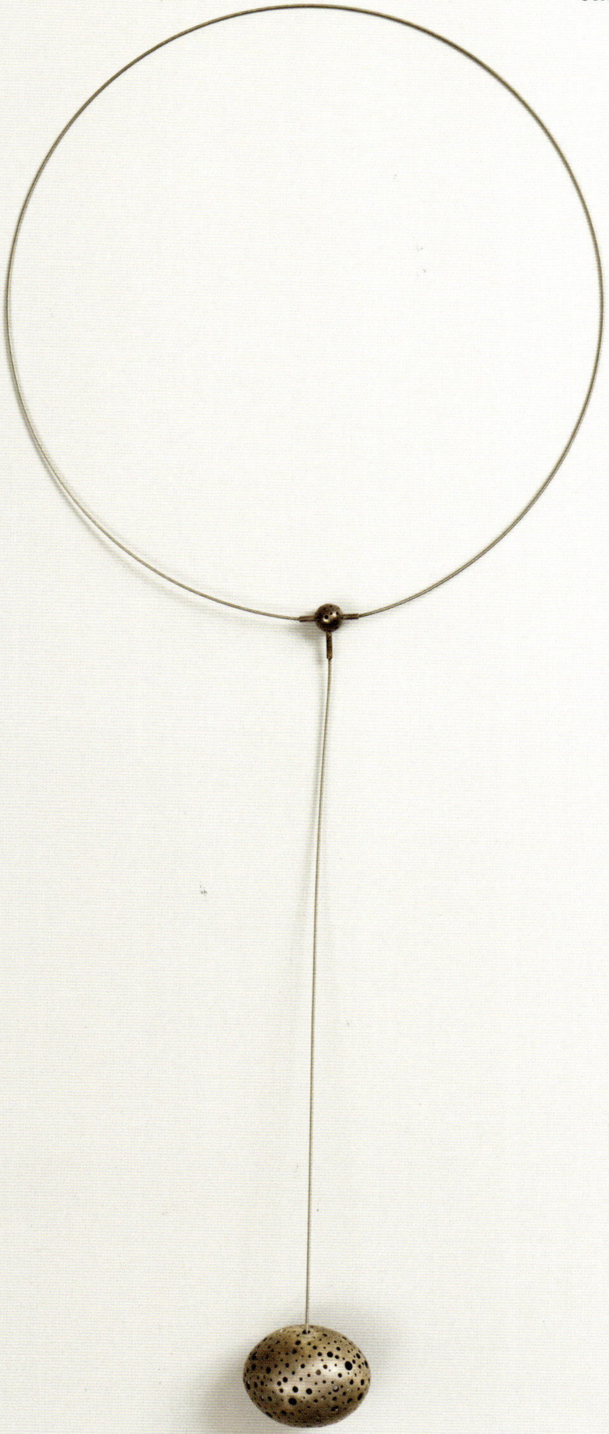

Sandra Enterline

Double Cylinder
Pendant Necklace;
2008

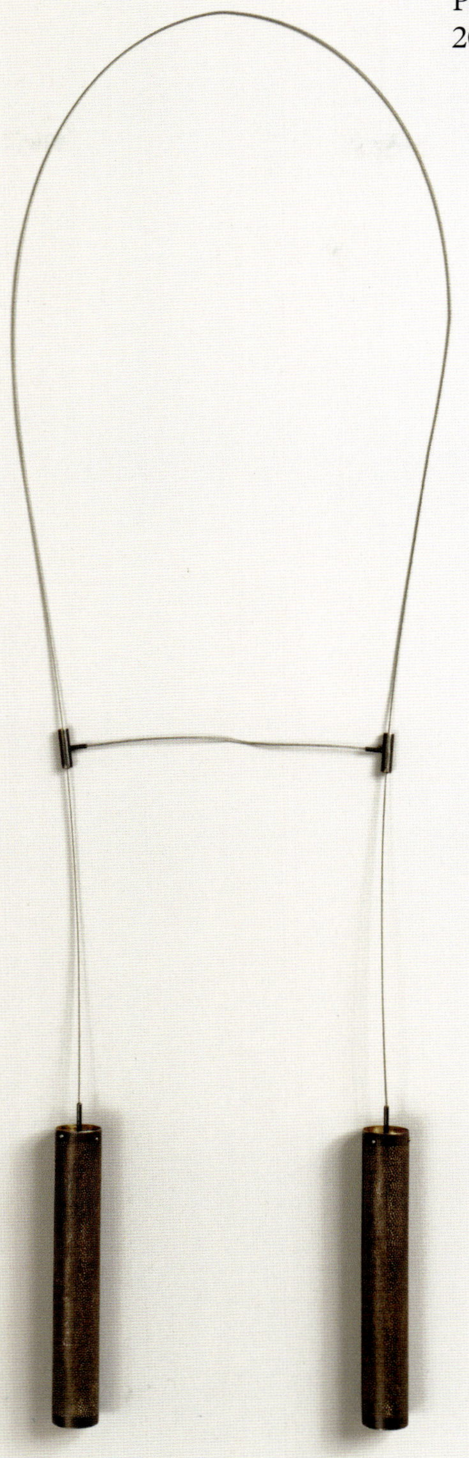

Bruno Martinazzi

Due Respiri Necklace,
2005

Manfred Bischoff
Brooch; 1987
(front, back)

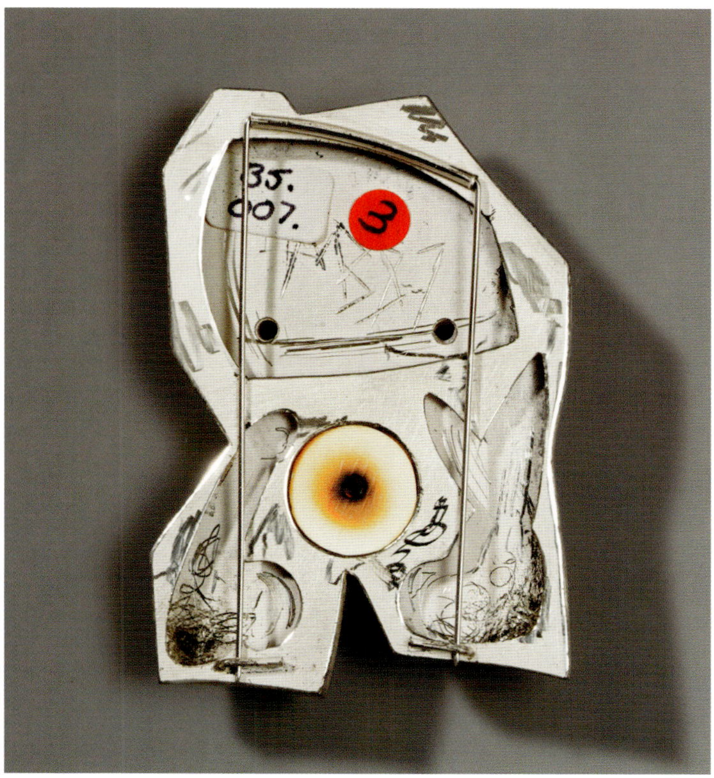

Katja Prins

Brooch from the Continuum Series; 2007

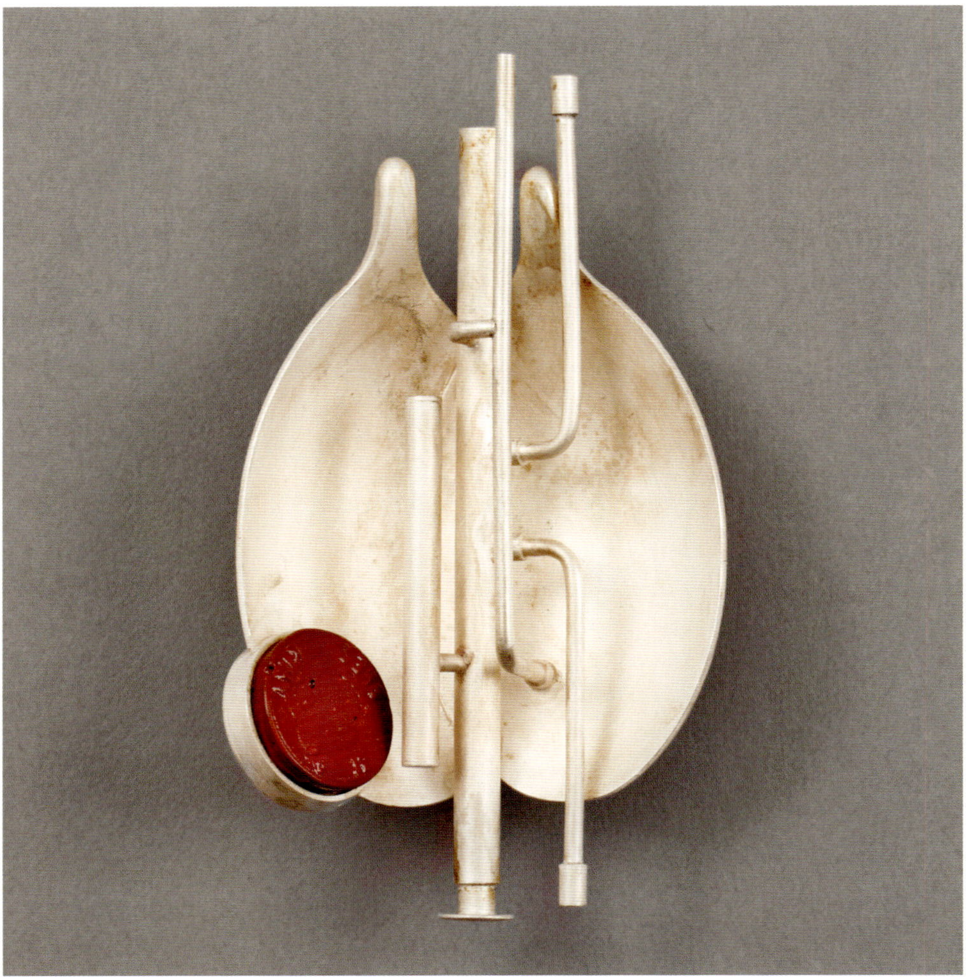

Doug Bucci

Black Sectional Necklace
from the Islet Series
2011

X Brooch, Bracelets and Tiara from the Candy Wear Series, 1999–2001

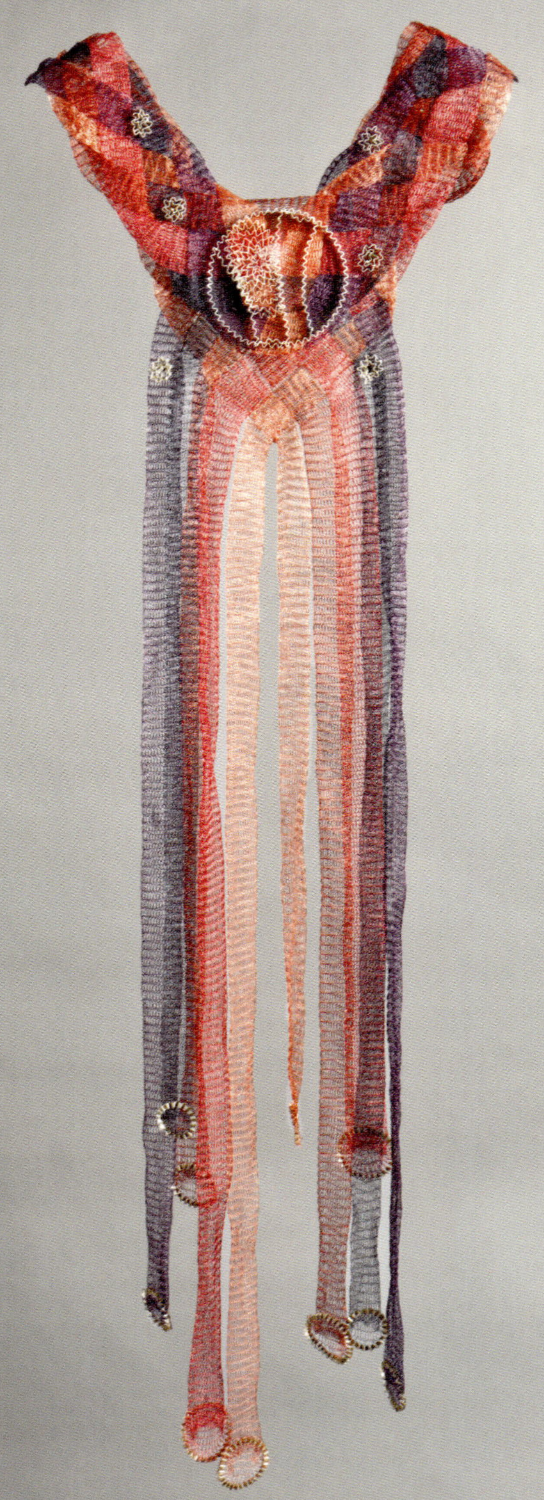

Arline Fisch

Multicolor Braid
with Silver Flowers
Necklace/Body Ornament;
1995 (full view and detail)

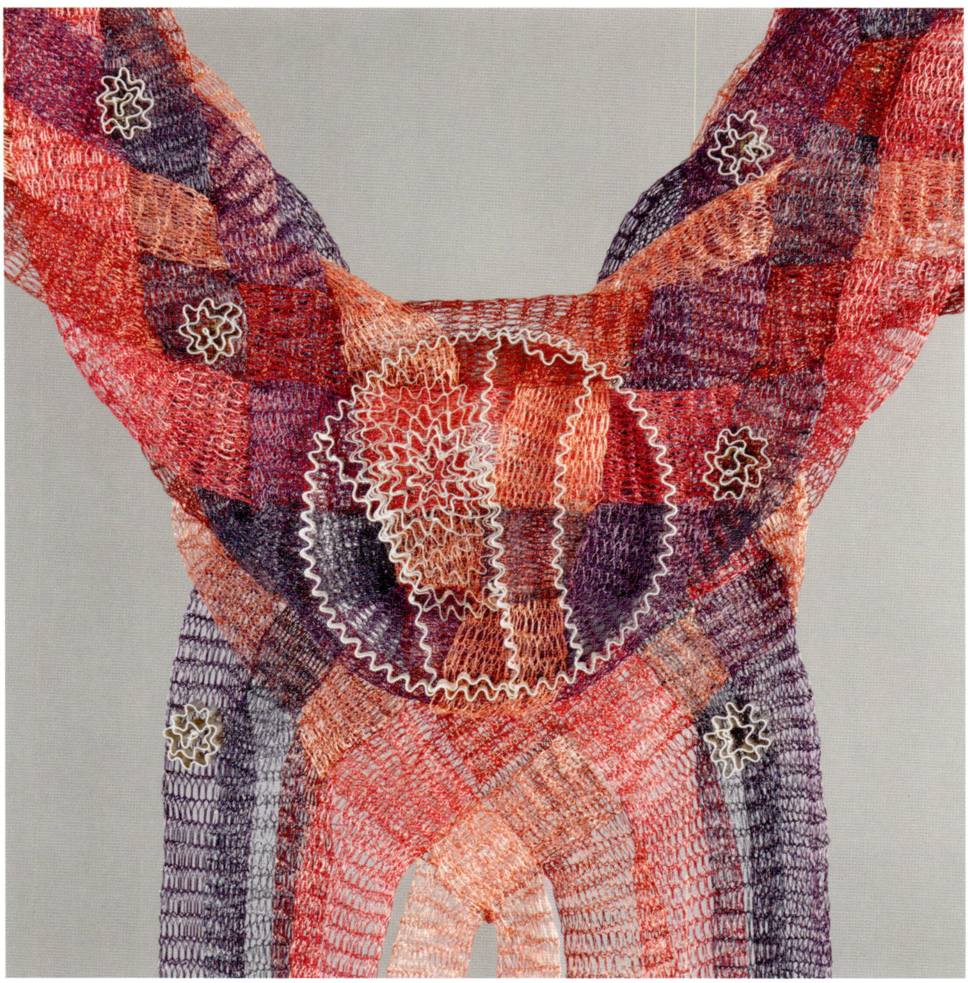

Axel Russmeyer

Tropical Punch Necklace;
2006

Felieke van der Leest

Object with Ring/Grey Heron Airplane Ring; 2006

Set of three Brooches and Holder from the *Heimat* (Home) Series; 2004

Esther Knobel

Print, The Mind in the Hand; 2006

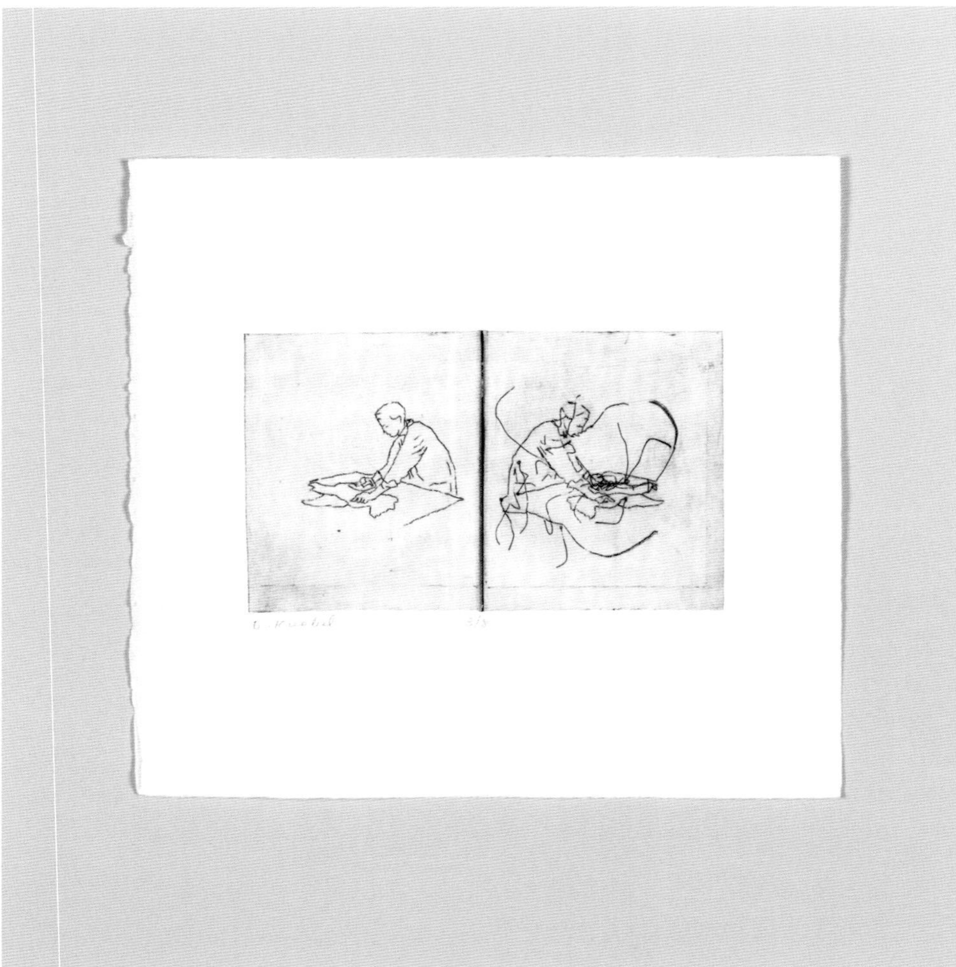

Esther Knobel

Brooch from The Mind in the Hand Series, 2007

Joyce Scott

Necklace; 2000s

Esther Knobel

Brooch from the Immigrant Series; ca. 1995

Iris Eichenberg

Brooch from the *Weiss* (White) Series; 2009

Deganit Stern Schocken

Necklace from the Kalandia Checkpoint Series, 2007

Kiff Slemmons

Reliquary of My Own Making Necklace; 2008

Giampaolo Babetto

Brooch;
1995

Abstract Forms

Abstract jewelry may be based upon primary shapes made from precious metals or from industrial materials. Other pieces might be biomorphic in form, curving with soft lines constructed from natural materials, or may reflect a painterly approach that highlights colors and patterns. In any configuration, this jewelry emphasizes the beauty found in non-representational shapes, and opens the mind to new interpretations suggested by pure formal considerations.

Giampaolo Babetto

Ring;
1995

Giampaolo Babetto

Ring
1981

Francesco Pavan

Brooch;
ca. 1985

Renzo Pasquale

Cono Brooch;
2015

Graziano Visintin

Drawing, Designs for a Brooch; 2002

Graziano Visintin

Brooch;
2002

Annamaria Zanella

Roofs Brooch;
2002

Annamaria Zanella
Drawings, Designs for
Roofs Brooch; 2002

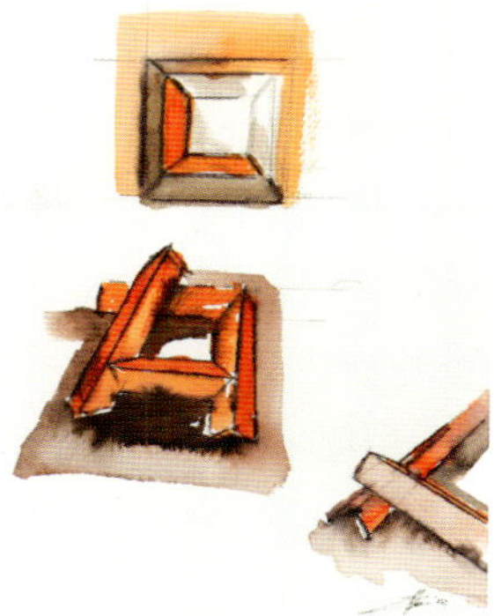

Anton Cepka

Brooch;
1998

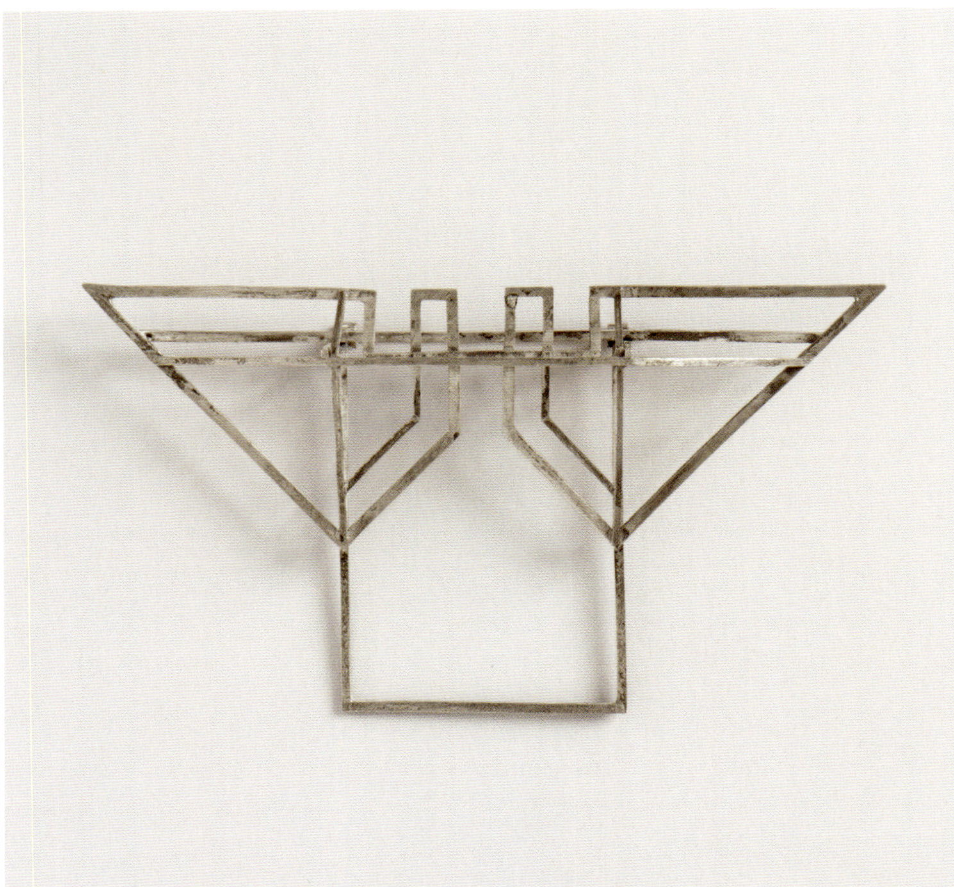

Peter Skubic

Brooch from the Mirror Brooches Series; 2001

Eva Eisler

Brooch from the Tension and Slate Series; 1991

Eva Eisler

Necklace from the Spring Steel Series; 2002

Lella Vignelli
Necklace; ca. 2000

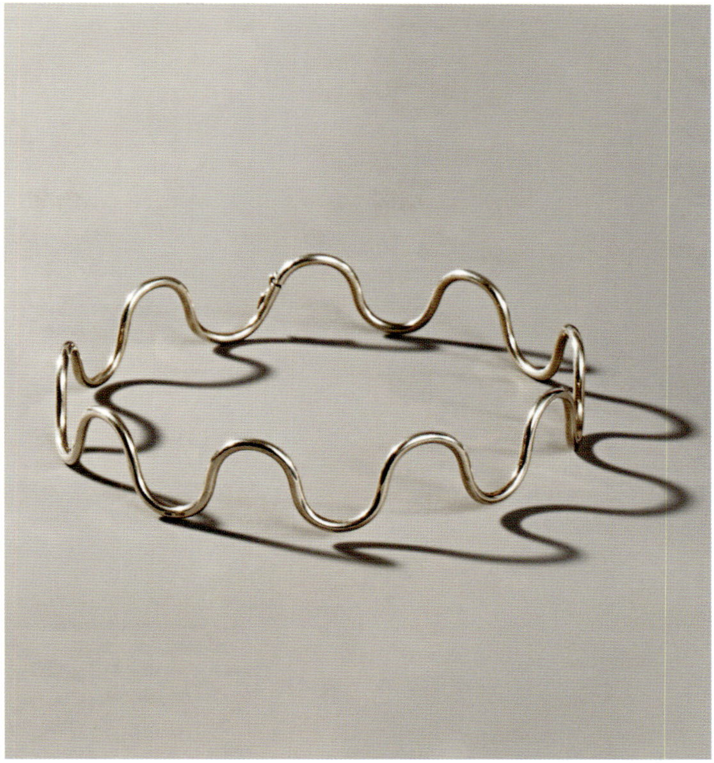

Jiří Šibor
Brooch from
the Twisted Circles
Series; 2001

Jiro Kamata

Brooch from the
Palette Series: 2015

Dorothea Prühl

Flyer Necklace;
2010

Bruce Metcalf

Fulfillment Necklace;
2004

Kazumi Nagano

Brooch;
2015

Kyoko Fukuchi

Brooch;
ca. 2013

Peter Hoogeboom

Desert Necklace from the Handle with Care Series; 1995

Gaetano Pesce
Bracelet; 2009

Myra Mimlitsch-Gray
Corners Necklace from the Molten Jewelry Series; 2006

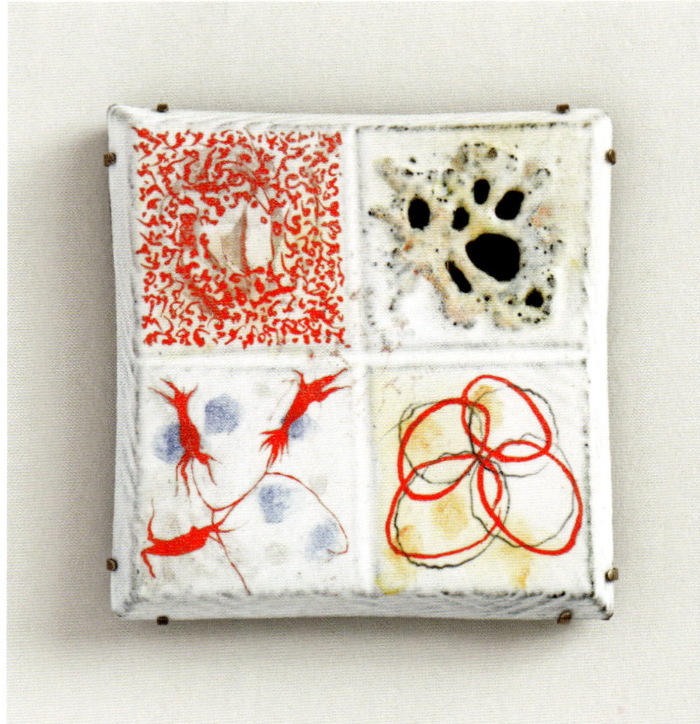

Jamie Bennett
Postpriori II Brooch
from the Postpriori
Series; 2008

Jamie Bennett
Drawing related to
Postpriori II Brooch;
2008

Karen Pontoppidan

Brooch from the Canvas Series; 2014

Thomas Gentille
Not titled8 Brooch;
Twentieth Century

Thomas Gentille
Drawing, Study in
Color and Form;
Twenty-First Century

Thomas Gentille
Not titled7
Two Part Brooch;
Twentieth Century

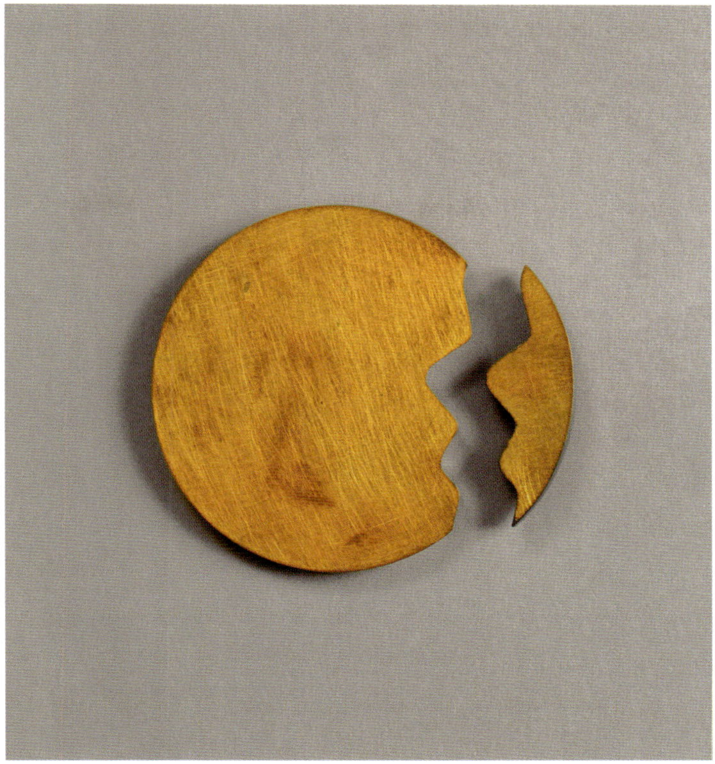

Thomas Gentille
Not titled Brooch
(DeMarco Series);
Twentieth Century

Ted Noten

Necklace from the Fred Pendant Series; 2003

Conceptual Jewelry

Traditional jewelry is often defined by its physical form and materials. This notion is abandoned when a concept defines a piece. Conceptual jewelry emphasizes intellectual ideas and the context in which jewelry functions. In creating such jewelry, makers may flirt with controversy. Their designs question and subvert jewelry's conventions and value systems, revealing alternative meanings, challenging the purpose of jewelry, and re-examining beliefs that surround symbols of wealth, status, and cultural identity.

Otto Künzli
The Manhattan Piece
Smoking Jewelry;
1987

Index of Works and Jewelers' Statements
Introduction by Thomas Gentille

Once upon a time, a very long time ago, the twelve-year old daughter of friends asked me, while sitting around the dining room having lunch, "What is jewelry? How do you make it?"

I suggested, when we've finished our meal, if she would like to, let's take a walk in the backyard and I'll show you how, and so we did. I asked her to gather anything that she especially liked, twigs, stones, feathers, weeds, flowers, anything. Elisabeth, for that was her name, gathered from her favorite tree, nine beautiful large green maple leaves.

I asked her if that was all she wanted, and she with great wisdom replied, "That is all I need."

We went into the house and I asked her mother Shirley for some string. From upstairs her father, Bill, brought down a ball of finely spun bright orange yarn that his wife Shirley had given him for us. Elisabeth and I carefully made some little holes in the maple leaves, next to the stems where the leaves are stronger. Between small knots we strung them, one by one, overlapping a little bit. I tied them over her shoulders with a little bow on the back of the neck and said to her that is what jewelry is and that's how you make it. She wore her emerald green necklace, with great contentment for the rest of the day.

Elisabeth spoke about her necklace every time I came back to visit. When I asked if she had kept it she said, "No, I liked it best when it was fresh and green. I like, very much, the memory of it, and anyhow I can always make a new one."

That small, very real afternoon of what seems like a fairy tale, has taken on nearly mythic proportions in my mind. For I often wonder if this is how jewelry began. The gathering of organic things somehow held together. Always with the desire to have the chosen objects made wearable in some way. Whatever the root of this desire, this need, to wear or adorn us with something other than clothing, it has held on to the human psyche warmly and gently. Much to our pleasure it has happily never let go.

Brooch (Italy), 1995; Molded, pressed, folded and stippled 18kt gold sheet with applied pigment; 6.2 × 4 × 2.6 cm (2 7/16 in. × 1 9/16 in. × 1 in.); 2016-34-1

Ring (Italy), 1995; Gold with applied white resin; 2 × 3.5 × 4 cm (13/16 × 1 3/8 × 1 9/16 in.); 2016-34-2

Giampaolo Babetto
(Italian, b. 1947)
[Clockwise: PP. 28, 100; 102, 103]

I've always avoided any sort of decoration in my work, I've always wanted a clean form, not so much to discover a geometrical or mathematic process behind the form, but because pure. . . forms . . . suit me, and I try to make them sensitive, to communicate something of myself to these forms.[1]

Ring (Italy), 1981; Gold; 2.5 × 4 × 4 cm (1 in. × 1 9/16 in. × 1 9/16 in.); 2016-34-3

Blinker Brooch from the Sportfiguren (Sports Figures) Series (Amsterdam, The Netherlands), 1988; Executed by Tobias van Roojen (Dutch); Gold, aquamarine, PVC-laminated newspaper; 16.5 × 6.3 × 1.9 cm (6 1/2 × 2 9/16 × 11/16 in.); 2016-34-4

Gijs Bakker
(Dutch, b. 1942)
[PP. 4, 26]

"I have always loved precious stones, but never found a good reason to use them until 1985. Fascinated by the images of soccer players in my daily newspaper, I combined an image of Regi Blinker—Dutch national team player—with an aquamarine replacing the soccer ball. Combining poor material (newspaper) with precious stones was a hit!"

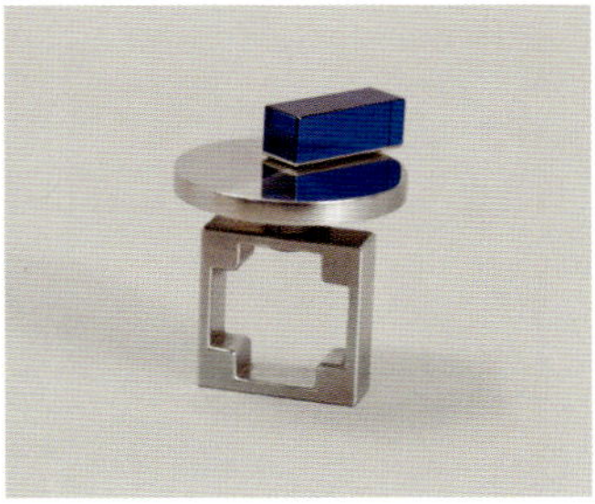

Kinetic Ring (Germany), 1993; Silver, acrylic; 3.5 × 3.2 cm (1 3/8 × 1 1/4 in.); 2016-34-5

Friedrich Becker
(German, 1922–1997)
[PP. 17, 55]

My ambition was to create my own designs, to research the rules of physics and to work empirically. My desire was to develop kinetics in jewelry on a miniature scale as well as in large scale objects, and herein lies my actual work and passion.

Becker's wife adds, "My husband always said, 'Our world is so chaotic, I wish that one day it will be brought back into balance.' This idea is fundamental to his kinetic work." [2]

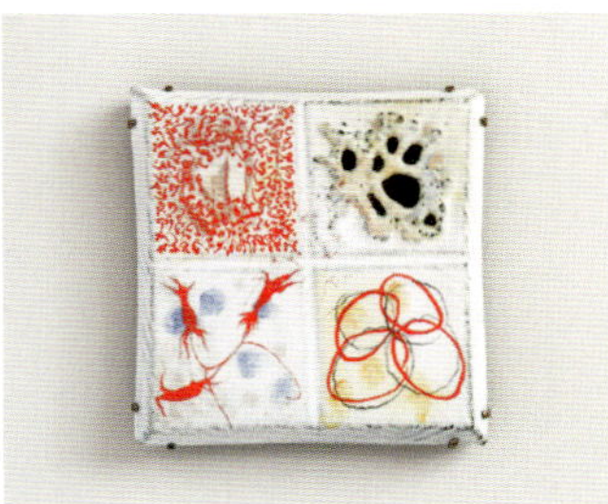

Postpriori II Brooch from the Postpriori Series (Stone Ridge, New York, USA), 2008; Enamel on electroformed copper, silver, gold; 6.5 × 6.5 × 1.3 cm (2 9/16 × 2 9/16 × 1/2 in.); 2016-34-6

Jamie Bennett
(American, b. 1948)
[P. 33]

"I'm interested in how cultures portray nature as an explanation of beauty. What I characterize as beauty has shifted from an integrated ornamental condition to a more incidental bodily appearance. The materials are critical to the physical character of the work and the resulting experience for the viewer. How things appear to us is the result of our value systems, and I am interested in representing what I value."

Bracelet (Munich, Germany), 1997; Sawn sheet plastic bands (Hosta-glas) wrapped in iron wire; 3.5 × 7.1 cm (1 3/8 × 2 13/16 in.); 2016-34-7

Doris Betz
(German, b. 1960)

"In 1997, I received a scholarship to work with a new plastic material called Hostaglas that had been developed for use in industrial products. This bracelet was made by fixing a strip of Hostaglas with more than 10 meters of iron wire in a way that the wire becomes ornamental. The big challenge was winding the wire without breaking it or ending up with a wire mess. Everything is visible in this piece—no place to hide anything."

Garlic (*Knoblauch*) Pendant Necklace (Munich, Germany), 2009; Folded sheet silver; 59 × 5 × 4.6 cm (23 1/4 × 1 15/16 × 1 13/16 in.); 2016-34-8

David Bielander
(Swiss, b. 1968)
[PP. 23, 75]

"I aim to walk a fine line between making something that is simple enough that one recognizes it and abstract enough that one has room for shifts in perception when engaging with it. The ambivalence occurs the moment the garlic is worn. Where does one belong when one wears such a piece? Where does the jewelry belong? How is it different from a head of garlic at the market? A moiré effect is what I want—a shimmer that is beautiful and seductive and delightful but can't be sorted out and arranged."

Brooch (probably Tuscany, Italy), 1987; Gold, cut coral; 6.5 × 4.5 × 1.2 cm (2 9/16 × 1 3/4 × 1/2 in.); 2016-34-10

Manfred Bischoff
(German, 1942–2015)
[PP. 24, 81]

Anyone who is creative should search for the right material to express his ideas, and in my case it's gold. I can't use pure gold. The metal has to have a certain hardness for me to work with it, so I have to settle for 22k gold. I don't have to do anything to clean it. It's like clear water. Gold 'goldens,' and I can get very, very foolish, controlled foolish, by making something in gold.[3]

Necklace from the Ingredients Series (Germany), 2008; Pyrite, glass, gold, wool, Kevlar; 24.5 × 22 × 3 cm (9 5/8 × 8 11/16 × 1 3/16 in.); 2016-34-11

Iris Bodemer
(German, b. 1970)

"The necklace is part of my Ingredients series in which objects and materials are assembled and forced together though sometimes have little in common. Attraction and rejection occur as energy is exchanged and contradictions and polarities are worked out mentally and actually. Hard, brittle pyrite, and fragile glass drops hang in the manner of suspended Easter eggs, waiting to break—or not."

Bracelet from the *Dekorationswut* Series (Germany), 2013; Silver, enamel, mirrors, paint; 7 × 8.5 × 3.6 cm (2 3/4 × 3 3/8 × 1 7/16 in.); 2016-34-12

Ring from the *Dekorationswut* Series (Germany), 2013; Oxidized silver, Swarovski chain, lacquer; 5.5 × 5 × 4.5 cm (2 3/16 × 1 15/16 × 1 3/4 in.); 2016-34-13

Coldstar Necklace from the *Dekorationswut* Series (Australia), 2012; Silver, molded plastic, paint; 41 × 18 × 0.9 cm (16 1/8 × 7 1/16 × 3/8 in.); Promised gift

Helen Britton
(Australian, b. 1966)
[Top Left and Right: PP. 19, 58, 59, Bottom: P. 74]

"My work in the studio is a process of direct, intuitive integration and construction, an open-ended experiment. I don't try to dictate what the work will say. I am conscious of what I have chosen to incorporate but am completely immersed in my own process of reinvention, in creation that lies well outside the limited boundaries of verbalization.

It is always challenging to give materials that are associated with popular culture and costume jewelry (mirrors, chains, plastics) a new life that references their history, but places them in a new genre, one that celebrates popular culture, but also moves beyond the usual, creating an object that questions our values but that still remains jewelry. The vibrating point between all these concerns is where the piece must arrive in the end, and to bring the piece to this point is the greatest and most interesting challenge."

Black Sectional Necklace from the Islet Series (Philadelphia, Pennsylvania, USA), 2011; 3D-printed glass-filled nylon, sterling silver; 5.4 x 36 cm (2 1/8 x 14 3/16 in.); Promised gift

Doug Bucci
(American, b. 1971)
[PP. 25, 83]

"This neckpiece was generated from a diabetic's collection of blood glucose readings. The collected data was transmitted from a continuous glucose-monitoring system and wirelessly streamed in 3D modeling software. The actualized form was sent to a 3D printer and directly manufactured layer by layer until the form had fused in its entirety. The finished neckpiece was then carefully extracted from the bed of the printer, much as an archaeologist extracts a fossil from the earth that surrounds the object. The final piece is a hand-dyed nylon form."

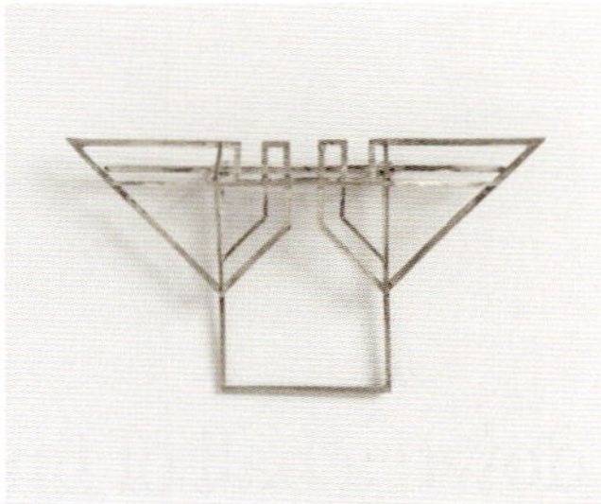

Brooch (Bratislava, Slovakia), 1998; Sawn and mounted silver; 5.1 × 10.5 × 2.1 cm (2 × 4 1/8 × 13/16 in.); 2016-34-14

Anton Cepka
(Slovakian, b. 1936)
[P. 30]

Untitled (5) Necklace from the Compounding Fractions Series (Germany), 2010; Paper, paint, coal, glue, linen; 20.5 × 15 × 7.3 cm (8 1/16 × 5 7/8 × 2 7/8 in.); 2016-34-15

Attai Chen
(Israeli, b. 1979)
[PP. 24, 77]

"It was my intention in this work to trace, create, and preserve the natural cycle of growth, culmination, consummation, decay, and growth again, not only through the form that I chose to make but also through the material that I chose to work with. The paper contains within itself the beauty and fragility of the moment. The form of the piece was created to preserve and reflect these feelings and ideas."

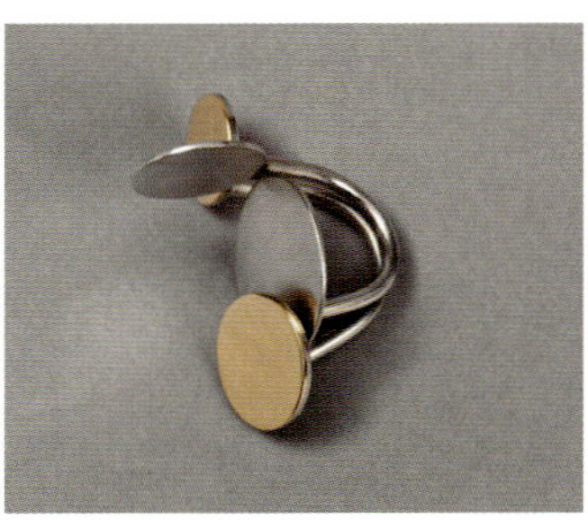

Ring (Baltimore, Maryland, USA), 1985; Silver, gold; 4 × 5.3 × 3 cm (1 9/16 × 2 1/16 × 1 3/16 in.); 2016-34-16

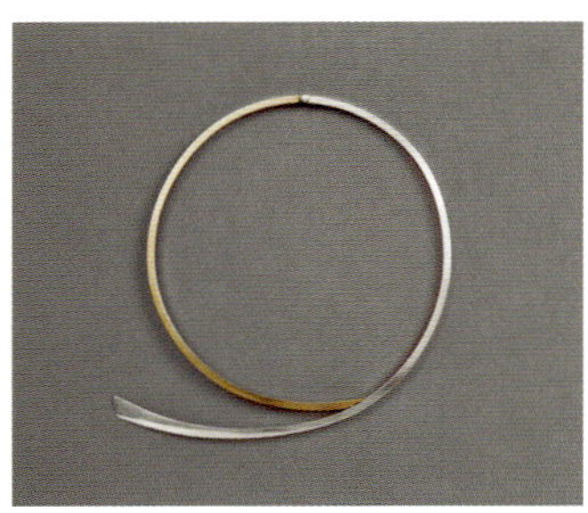

Necklace (Baltimore, Maryland, USA), 1948; Silver, brass; 13.9 × 14 × 0.8 cm (5 1/2 × 5 1/2 × 5/16 in.); 2017-2-1

Betty Cooke
(American, b. 1924)
[Left: P. 45, Right: PP. 14, 44]

"The challenge for me is for the final object to express my original vision and style and for it to reflect the high design standards I have set for myself. That's exciting and personally rewarding."

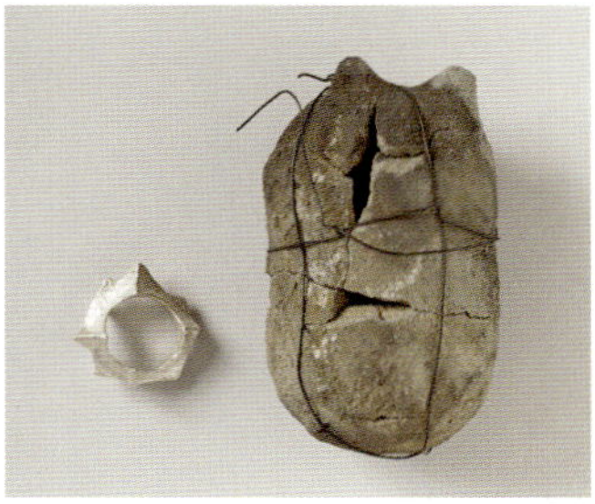

Ring and mold from the fast ASHANTI Series (Switzerland), 2002; Cast silver (closed cycle technique) (ring), clay (mold); Ring: 1.6 × 3.1 cm (5/8 × 1 1/4 in.), Mold: 9.7 × 5.3 cm (3 13/16 × 2 1/16 in.); 2016-34-17-a/c

Johanna Dahm
(Swiss, b. 1947)
[P. 64]

"The ring was modeled in clay in the negative and cast in the abbreviated "closed cycle" casting technique of the Ashanti in Ghana and the Dokra in India."

Ring from the NY NY. . . right before my eyes Series (Jersey City, New Jersey, USA), 2009; Electroformed copper on stones and earth; 4 × 3 × 2 cm (1 × 1 3/16 × 3/16 in.); Promised gift

Necklace from the Found at. . . Made in. . . Series (Caleta Brecknock, Chile), 2015; Wood, beads, rope, polymer clay (porcelana fria); 44 × 14 × 3.4 cm (17 5/16 × 5 1/2 × 1 5/16 in.); 2016-34-18

Rian de Jong
(Dutch, b. 1951)
[Left: P. 56]

"Through my travels as a sailor, I have learned to look for forms, colors, and "found" objects, which I then process into wearable pieces. The challenge is to produce these pieces using the limited choices on board. I believe that my work is not so much "made" as formed by my curiosity about both material and technique. It is this curiosity that allows me to be anywhere in the world and be inspired by all that is around me."

Ring from the FOREVERRING Series (Germany), 2007; Hammered and patinated copper; 0.9 × 2.7 cm (3/8 × 1 1/16 in.); 2017-4-1

Bettina Dittlmann
(German, b. 1964)

Michael Jank
(German, b. 1972)

"Since 1999, we have made over two thousand "forever rings," forging them out of pure gold, pure silver, copper, and iron. We work together, but also separately, passing pieces back and forth to one another until, in the end, it would be impossible to say which of us is responsible for any particular aspect of the ring, which of us made an imprint with the hammer. The most challenging part is knowing when a ring is finished."

Brooch from the Ginger Series (Germany), 2004; Electroformed silver; 4.8 × 6.4 × 2 cm (1 3/4 × 2 1/4 × 1 in.); 2016-34-110

Sam Tho Duong
(Vietnamese, b. 1969)
[P. 23]

"Ginger looks like a simple root, but it is both spicy and sweet, and it comes in many forms. It is used as a condiment for exotic dishes as well as the basis for ginger bread and ginger ale. My necklaces and brooches are part of a series of objects made from one piece of ginger root, and materials such as copper, silver, and gold, with additional surface treatments that include enamel, pearls, and stones. They are like sisters and brothers with different characters."

Necklace from the ColorCore Personal Adornment Series (New Paltz, New York, USA), 1983; ColorCore Formica fragments, clothespins (painted wood, metal), cord; L x W x D: 36.3 × 26.4 × 1.3 cm (14 5/16 × 10 3/8 × 1/2 in.); 2016-34-19

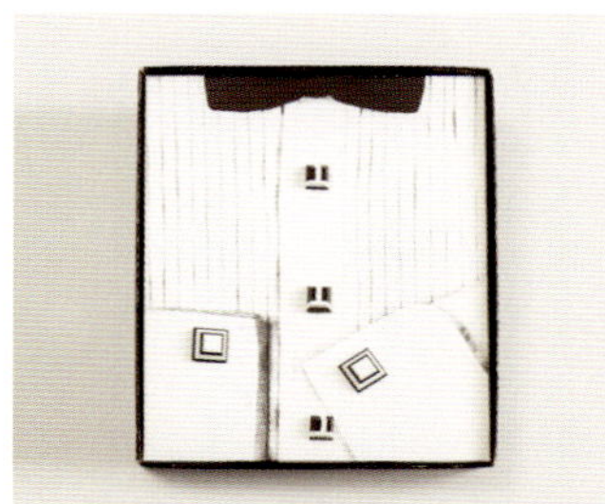

Pair of Cufflinks and Three Studs with Packaging from the ColorCore Personal Adornment Series (New Paltz, New York, USA), 1983; ColorCore Formica; (cufflinks, studs); printed cardboard (packaging); 2.7 × 15.5 × 18 cm (1 1/16 × 6 1/8 × 7 1/16 in.); 2016-34-20-a/f

Robert Ebendorf
(American, b. 1938)

Ivy Ross
(American, b. 1955)
[Left: PP. 15, 48]

"For the ColorCore project, each object was designed by Ivy Ross but hand-built by me. The challenging aspect was working with a totally inflexible material that shatters like glass when you break it, but the idea of fractured edges and hard edges appealed to me. For the cufflinks and studs, we stacked the laminate in alternating black and white layers, and Ivy, who was familiar with the fashion world and marketing, designed packaging for them."

Brooch from the *Weiss* (White) Series (The Netherlands), 2009; Silver, porcelain, leather, thread; 20 × 7 × 3 cm (7 7/8 × 2 3/4 × 1 3/16 in.); 2016-34-21

Bird Slip-on Brooch from the Black Birds Series (The Netherlands), 2012; Sheet copper, electroformed copper, ribbon (silk); 9 × 14.5 × 4.2 cm (3 9/16 × 5 11/16 × 1 5/8 in.); 2016-34-22

Iris Eichenberg
(German, b. 1965)
[Top Left: P. 27, Bottom Left: P. 26]

Weiss – This work embodies interrelations in different forms. The visual complexity, the variety of materials reflects the complexity of chosen relations. The oval forms, in which a face or body contour may be projected, show that such systems revolve around people. The systems that connect them may take on all kinds of shapes, but they eventually function because of the human elements that give them meaning.[5]

(Works continue on page 141.)

Set of Three Brooches and Holder from the *Heimat* (Home) Series (The Netherlands), 2004; Metal, thread skeins, cardboard (box); 6 × 25.1 × 18.3 cm (2 3/8 × 9 7/8 × 7 3/16 in.); 2016-34-23-a/s

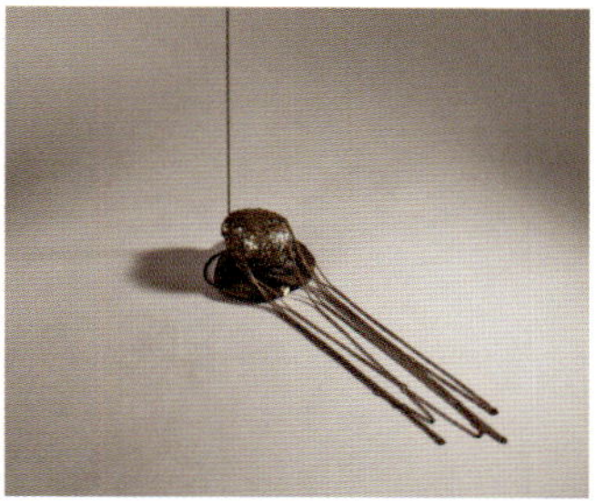

Necklace and Stand from the X Series (The Netherlands), 2014–15; Oxidized nails, metal wire, silver, steel, wood, Perspex; 64 × 12 × 36 cm (25 3/16 × 4 3/4 × 14 3/16 in.); Promised gift

Heimat – One of those untranslatable German words that crossed boundaries and found its way into other languages, heimat is associated with origins, home, or a space/time ridden with desire and longing. Each of Eichenberg's works embodies a quest for meaning. Does meaning reside in materials, or does it arise from the handling, contextualizing, and reflecting upon them? These works suggest universal questions about belonging, being and becoming.[4]

Necklace from the Spring Steel Series (New York, New York, USA), 2002; 1.7 × 20 cm (11/16 × 7 7/8 in.); 2016-34-24

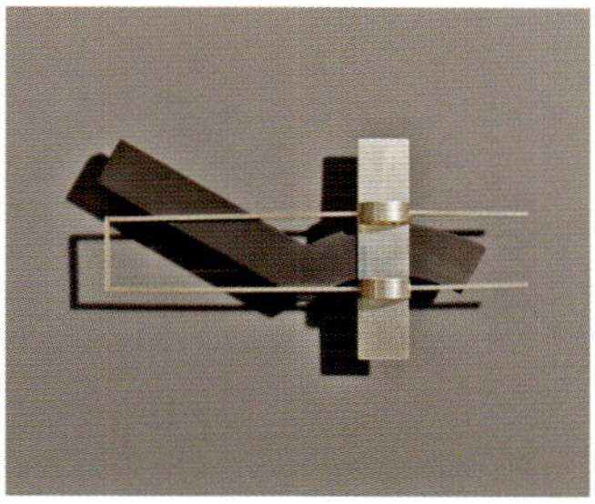

Brooch from the Tension and Slate Series (New York, New York, USA), 1991; Assembled and cold connection-constructed silver and slate; 13.7 × 7 × 2.3 cm (5 3/8 × 2 3/4 × 7/8 in.); 2016-34-25

Eva Eisler
(Czech/English, b. Prague, 1952)
[Both P. 30, Left P. 114, Right PP. 112-113]

"The necklaces in my Spring Steel series were inspired by simple paper chains and made from constant-force stainless steel flat springs. The combination of silver or steel and the dark gray color of the stone in an open configuration of geometrical/architectural forms enables the wearer to feel a part of the contemporary environment."

Egg Pendant Necklace (San Francisco, California, USA), ca. 1991; Hollow-formed and fabricated silver and stainless steel; 45 × 19.6 × 3 cm (17 11/16 × 7 11/16 × 1 3/16 in.); 2016-34-26

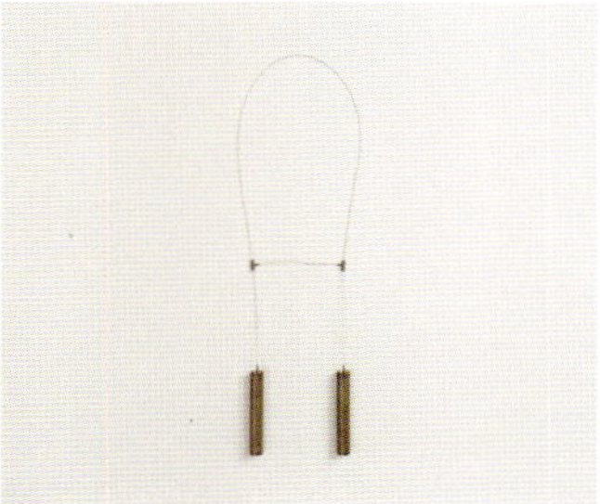

Double Cylinder Pendant Necklace (San Francisco, California, USA), 2008; Fabricated, oxidized sterling silver, hand-drilled and perforated gold and stainless steel; 50.7 × 11.7 × 1.5 cm (19 15/16 × 4 5/8 × 9/16 in.); 2016-34-27

Sandra Enterline
(American, b. 1960)
[Left to Right: P. 78, P. 79]

"**Double Cylinder Necklace** is based on the fascination with light when seen through hundreds of tiny perforations. There is a powerful interplay between the interior and exterior of the piece. The interior is concealed by the form, and revealed by the perforations. After perforating the pieces, I formed them into two cylinders, designing the mechanisms on the pendant, leaving the sculptural simplicity of the overall piece."

"**Egg Pendant** evolved out of my obsession with forming spheres in the late 1980s, which led to a series of egg pendants I made in the early 1990s."

Claire Falkenstein
(American, 1908–1997)
[Left and Right P. 12, Left P. 42]

Well, if you look at my work, of course there's some influence. You can't just go through life not being influenced at all. But there is a kind of action always in my work that is of a kind of interior growth, rather than exterior association with some style or some subject. I've always worked out my own direction.[6]

Necklace (USA), ca. 1965; Glass, bent, flattened, welded copper wire, leather; 39.2 × 12.5 × 3 cm (15 7/16 × 4 15/16 × 1 3/16 in.); 2016-34-28

Ring (USA), ca. 1955; Folded sheet silver, bent silver wire; 2.4 x 4 x 4.8 cm (15/16 x 1 9/16 x 1 7/8 in.); 2017-2-2

Arline Fisch
(American, b. 1931)
[Top Left and Right: P.14
Bottom: PP. 25, 86, 87]

"Knitting in metal is magical. An amorphous mass of looped wire mesh produced by the knitting process can be transformed in the hands. Pushing and pulling, stretching and compressing the elastic, pliable plane of the knitted structure results in an endless variety of sculptural forms that can be retained permanently. The transparency of the knitted structure allows for layerings of density, creating forms within forms and subtle changes of color."

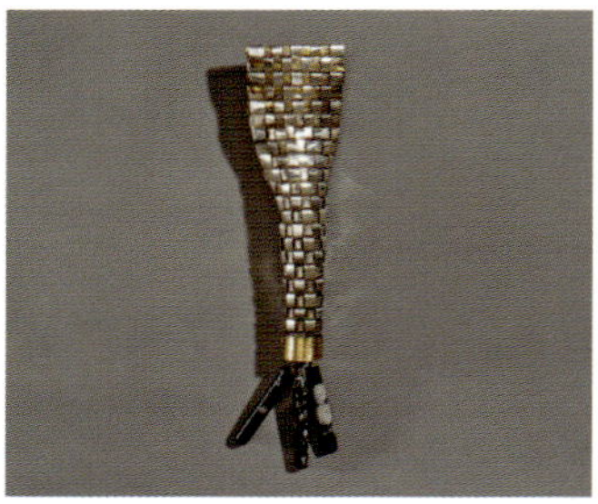

Spirit with 3 Legs Brooch from the Spirit Houses Series (USA), 1988; Woven silver and gold, agate; 15.1 x 6.6 × 1.2 cm (5 15/16 x 2 5/8 x 1/2 in.); 2016-34-29

Brooch (USA), 1984; Sheet silver, mosaic stone, rolled and compressed stainless steel mesh and knitted copper wire; 15.1 x 6.6 x 1.2 cm (5 15/16 × 2 5/8 × 1/2 in.); 2016-34-30

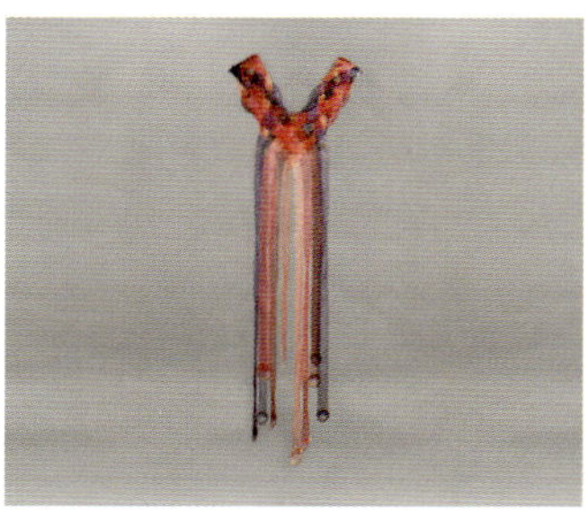

Multicolor Braid with Silver Flowers Necklace/Body Ornament (San Diego, California, USA), 1995; Machine-knitted tubes of coated copper wire, flattened, assembled and braided; applied silver embellishments; 115.57 x 35.6 x 7.62 cm (45 1/2 x 14 x 3 in.); 2016-34-31

Be Long in Coming Brooch from the *Dolomitensagen* Series (The Netherlands), 2008; Silver, resin, print; 6 × 9.2 × 1 cm (2 7/8 × 3 5/8 × 1/2 in.); 2016-34-32

Jantje Fleischhut
(German, b. 1972)
[PP. 22, 73]

An old legend about the Dolomites mountain range was the inspiration behind the jewelry of the *Dolomitensagen* series. The imagery in the series creates suggestive, abstract compositions, rather than direct views or landscapes. Drawings and photographs incorporated in multilayered images at different scales combine to produce mysterious and compelling perspectives.[7]

Rambutan Ring (England), 2003; Plastic, knitted, knotted and dyed nylon filament with black pearls; 14.5 x 5 x 3.5 cm (5 × 1 1/4 × 1 1/4 in.); 2016-34-33

Nora Fok
(English, b. Hong Kong, China, 1953)

"I spend a lot of time looking at the wonderful and weird structures and colors in the natural world. The rambutan, a Southeast Asian fruit, has intrigued me since I was a child and put one in my pocket, where it quickly turned black. I often work with nylon monofilament and could see the material's potential for interpreting my childhood experience. I knitted dyed nylon into a globe, knotted black pearls on the surface, and finished the fruit with nylon spikes."

Temptation Brooch from the Organic Series (Madison, Wisconsin, USA), 2013; Cast, ground, sandblasted, acid etched and polished glass, anodized niobium, cast and laser welded gold, fabricated silver and gold (setting); 6.3 × 6 × 1.4 cm (2 1/2 × 2 3/8 × 9/16 in.); 2016-34-34

Donald Friedlich
(American, b. 1954)

"Few things in the world are more important to me than food and humor, but I had never thought to bring either into my jewelry until now. For my whole career, I've worked abstractly and most often geometrically, so my recent organic series is a major departure for me. I find integrating glassworking and goldsmithing into one unified jewelry design to be the ultimate test of my technical and artistic skills."

Kyoko Fukuchi
(Japanese, b. 1946)
[P. 31]

Brooch (Japan), ca. 2013; Urushi lacquer; 9 × 7.7 × 2.8 cm (3 9/16 × 3 1/16 × 1 1/8 in.); Promised gift

"To form the brooch I made a model in wood, stuck hemp to it using urushi (lacquer) as glue, and painted the surface repeatedly in colored urushi.
To make a larger but lighter work I use a kanshitsu (dried urushi) technique: I first make a model in paper or hemp, then paint the surface repeatedly to make layers of urushi. Finally, I remove the model resulting in a hollow urushi form."

Thomas Gentille
(American, b. 1936)
[PP. 32, 126, 127]

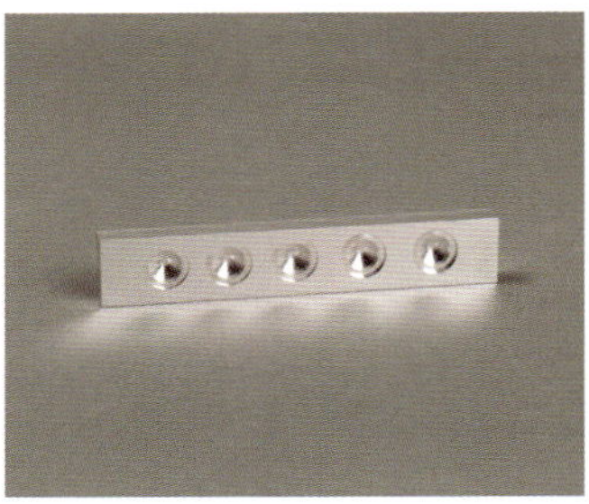

Not titled9 Brooch (USA), Twenty-first century; Aluminum; 2 × 11 × 1.5 cm (13/16 × 4 5/16 × 9/16 in.); 2016-34-35

Not titled8 Brooch (USA), Twentieth century; Eggshell inlay, metal; 13 × 9.3 × 2.3 cm (5 1/8 × 3 11/16 × 7/8 in.); 2016-34-36

Not titled Brooch (DeMarco Series) (USA), Twentieth century; Bronze, gold, paint; 0.5 x 7 cm (3/16 x 2 3/4 in.); 2016-34-37

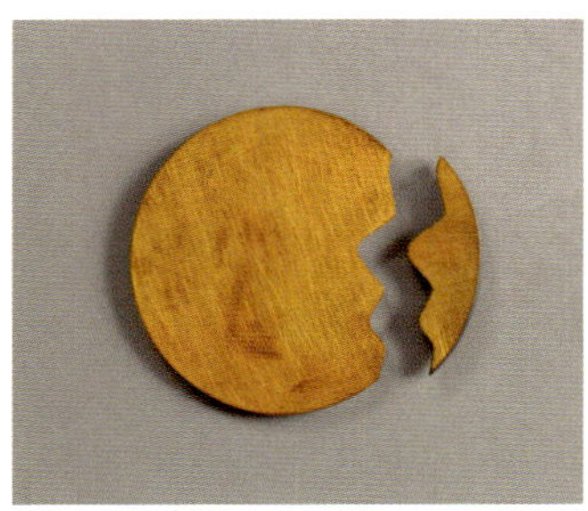

Not titled7 Brooch (USA), Twentieth century; Bronze, gold findings; 7.5 × 6.8 × 1 cm (2 15/16 × 2 11/16 × 3/8 in.) (part a), 5.5 × 1.9 × 1 cm (2 3/16 × 3/4 × 3/8 in.) (part b); 2016-34-38-a,b

Dieg Bou Diar 1 Necklace from the *Dieg Bou Diar* Series (Amsterdam, The Netherlands), 2006; Metal worked by Moussa Thiam (Senegalese), glass blown by Edwin Dieperink (Dutch); Steel, lamp-blown glass, silver, thread, magnet (closure); 3.5 × 24 cm (1 3/8 × 9 7/16 in.); Promised gift

Mieke Groot
(Dutch, b. 1949)
[PP. 20, 62-63]

"For the last forty years I have made objects in glass that are meant to be viewed and experienced as art, independently of their being worn on the body. Being a collector of ethnic jewelry from around the world, I am fascinated by its powerful shapes and symbolic value. The necklaces I make are cultural hybrids that express the many types of interactions that take place in the global community of object makers."

Wing Bracelet from the Winged Cuffs Series (USA), 2012; 3D-printed nylon; 8.2 × 13 × 13 cm (3 1/4 × 5 1/8 × 5 1/8 in.); 2016-34-39

Arthur Hash
(American, b. Panama, 1976)

"This piece was digitally "sculpted" and then 3D printed using Haptic-sensitive hardware and organic modeling software to create a one-of-a-kind wearable cuff. While most CAD-based software is driven by data/number entry, this particular workflow allows for the growth of geometry through the subtle movements of the mouse and varying pressures of a stylus nib. This "hands on" approach generates objects that can only be duplicated with real-world carving or sculpting."

Necklace from the What you say is not always what you have experienced Series (Stockholm, Sweden), 2009; Silver, powder-coated copper, paint; 47.2 × 12 × 5 cm (18 9/16 × 4 3/4 × 1 15/16 in.); 2016-34-40

Hanna Hedman
(Swedish, b. 1980)
[PP. 22, 68]

"I was inspired by an interest in storytelling and how stories change depending on the narrator. The development of each piece progressed with limited predefined planning. Fragments were created individually and then combined in a similar fashion as stories over time. Reality and dreams of past centuries meet in an ornamental story that is neither black nor white; instead it exists in a grey area; undefined and strange."

Padova Neckpiece (Doetinchem, The Netherlands), 1985; Stained, laminated, bent, sanded, and varnished birchwood; 22 × 24.5 × 5.6 cm (8 11/16 × 9 5/8 × 2 3/16 in.); 2016-34-41

Maria Hees
(Dutch, b. 1948)

"I wanted to make a wooden necklace that would follow the shape of the neck, so I began by staining thin layers of airplane plywood and gluing them together in a mold. Then I sawed out the shape, polished it, sanded it, and varnished it. The challenge was to make something that looked perfect in spite of the hard work required to achieve that effect."

Satellite Brooch from the Photo Brooches Series (The Netherlands), 2010; Aluminum dibond laminated photograph, plastic reflector, glass beads; 5.5 × 9.3 × 2.9 cm (2 (3/16 × 3 11/16 × 1 1/8 in); 2016-34-42

Ring from the Glassring Series (The Netherlands), 1986; Silver, glass; 3 × 3.6 × 3.5 cm (1 3/16 × 1 7/16 × 1 3/8 in.); 2016-34-43

Herman Hermsen
(Dutch, b. 1953)

"I began working with photographs in 2009, adding things to images in an attempt to introduce humor, create a particular atmosphere, or initiate fantasies. The picture in this brooch triggers a sense of receiving something undefined and sending reflected brilliance. Since I started out as a designer, the challenge for me in making jewelry is to express new concepts and new technical solutions through a contemporary interpretation of value and craft and through expressive and innovative design."

Only the Names Have Been Changed Brooch, one of a two-piece series (Munich, Germany), 2008; Cast gold; 7.2 × 7.7 × 1.1 cm (2 13/16 × 3 1/16 × 7/16 in.); 2016-34-44

Stefan Heuser
(German, b. 1978)

"I'm not the sort who spends hours making objects in search of an idea or a concept. Most of the time I start work with a title and a basic concept, and then I get around to making the material object. The true test of my idea is whether the finished piece suits me, whether I would like it for myself or for my girlfriend."

Desert Necklace from the Handle with Care Series (Amsterdam, The Netherlands), 1995; Slip cast and glazed ceramic, silver, cork; 23.7 × 17 × 5 cm (9 5/16 × 6 11/16 × 1 15/16 in.); 2016-34-45

Peter Hoogeboom
(Dutch, b. 1961)
[P. 122]

"I have always loved the look of ceramics, yet, even though museums have commonly shown ceramic neckpieces from antiquity, I wasn't seeing them in contemporary jewelry. I started to explore "new" material in the mid-nineties and learned that the great number of hollow elements that I would need to build my neckpieces could be produced easily through slip casting. Each piece in this series tells a story of vulnerability."

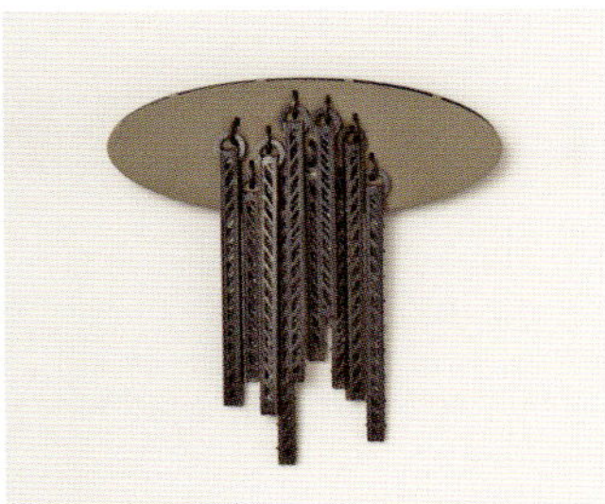

Cavea (23) Brooch from the Cavea Series (Munich, Germany), 2013; Laser-cut, folded, and constructed silver elements, enamel, crushed hematite, glimmer, lacquer; 12.4 × 13.2 × 2 cm (4 7/8 × 5 3/16 × 13/16 in.); Promised gift

Melanie Isverding
(German, b. 1978)

"Cavea suggests an enclosure or cage or exterior that protects its contents. Creating the filigree to express this idea required using a laser cutter, and mastering the technique was intense and difficult. In the end the effort was worth it. The laser cutter allowed me to articulate complex ideas about jewelry, materials, status, and symbolism and to realize that discovering the "new" was still an expression of my sensitivity and skill as a handmaker."

Brooch (USA), ca. 1995; Cast bronze; 15.9 × 10.8 × 1.1 cm (6 1/4 × 4 1/4 × 7/16 in.); 2016-34-46

John Iversen
(American, b. Germany, 1953)
[P. 23]

"My work with leaves continues to this day, evolving as I grow older. This piece is from the period when I realized that the metal itself is more beautiful than any polishing or finishing that can be done to it. The waxing, carving, and mechanics are on the back and the edges of the piece. The concept is in the vein of Duchamp's "readymades." Ideally there would be a tree growing jewelry."

Shield #3 Brooch from the Time Structures Series (Gardiner, New York, USA), 2005; Steel watch hands pressure-fitted around fabricated silver frame; 12.1 × 5.5 × 1.1 cm (5 × 2 in. × 1/2 in.); 2016-34-47

Knot Brooch from the Singularity Series (USA), 2007; Annealed and bent steel jeweler's saw blades, steel; 6.4 x 2 x 3 cm (2 1/2 x 13/16 x 1 3/16 in); 2017-34-48

Sergey Jivetin
(Uzbekistani, b. 1977)
[Left and Right: PP. 20, 21, 60]

"**Shield #3** – Time Structures series, explores a multitude of cultural associations imbued in tiny objects such as a simple watch hand. Each piece in the series utilizes a unique formal arrangement while expanding upon curious interconnections between man-made and animal-made defensive architectural structures."

"**Knot** explores the complex physical and ideological associations when one morphs into a mass of many. Saw blades are used to develop fractal texture. As each one is annealed and individually bent into a loop, the brooch volume and strength increase until the structure develops into a knot."

Bracelet from the Candy Wear Series (Cambridge, Massachusetts, USA), 1999; Electroformed, assembled, and soldered silver covered in electrostatically-applied rayon flocking bonded with adhesive; magnets; 4.3 × 13.5 cm (1 11/16 × 5 5/16 in.); 2016-34-49

Tiara from the Candy Wear Series (Cambridge, Massachusetts, USA), 2000; Copper, electroformed, assembled, and soldered silver covered in electrostatically-applied rayon flocking bonded with adhesive; 12.2 × 19.2 × 12 cm (4 13/16 × 7 9/16 × 4 3/4 in.); 2016-34-51

X Brooch and Two Bracelets from the Candy Wear Series (Cambridge, Massachusetts, USA), 2000-2001; Electroformed, assembled, and soldered silver covered in electrostatically-applied rayon flocking; Brooch: 6.5 × 6.5 × 1 cm (2 9/16 × 2 9/16 × 3/8 in.), Bracelets: 1.1 × 10 cm (7/16 × 3 15/16 in.); 2016-34-50-a/c

Daniel Jocz
(American, b. 1943)
[All: PP. 25, 84-85]

"Making Candy Wear involved a demanding process with exacting standards each step of the way in order to produce hollow pieces with electroformed silver surfaces suitable for flocking. The final assembly, soldering, flocking, fitting, and finishing of the pieces was done in my studio, with rayon flocking fibers electrostatically applied to a heat-cured adhesive on the silver, and magnets set into the clasps."

Lavendoux Brooch (Berlin, Germany), 2002; Water jet-cut, surface-treated, hand-colored, crafted polycarbonate (Makrofol); 10 × 8.6 × 7.6 cm (3 15/16 × 3 3/8 in × 3 in.); 2016-34-53

Svenja John
(German, b. 1963)
[P. 31]

"Since 1992, I have been working with a technical polycarbonate film. This industrial plastic provides stability and flexibility. The starting point for my works is a colorless film. Over and over again, I become fascinated with the possibility of transforming the film into three-dimensional forms and giving the sober material a fascinating character that lies somewhere between technical rigor and natural opulence. I modify the plastic by applying a delicate coloring."

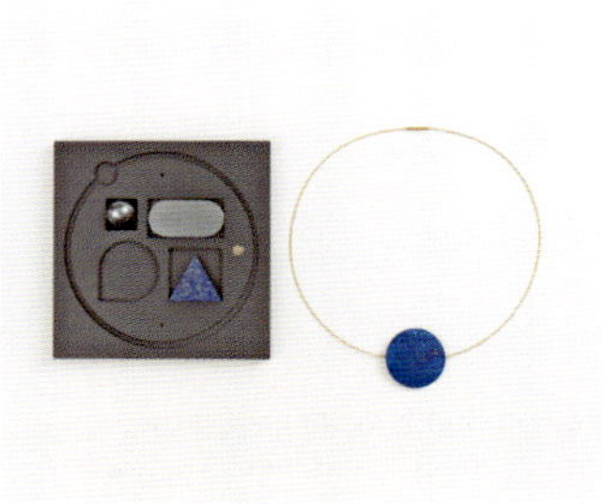

Necklace with Pendants and Box from *Serie Kasten* (the Box Series) (Munich, Germany), 1993; Lapis lazuli, hematite, gold, painted wood (case); (case open): 2.3 × 15.6 × 29.1 cm (7/8 × 6 1/8 × 11 7/16 in.); 2016-34-54-a/f

Necklace from *Serie Anhänger* (the Pendant Series) (Germany); 1994; Gold; 36.6 × 11.5 × 8 cm (14 7/16 × 4 1/2 × 3 1/8 in.); 2016-34-55

Hermann Jünger
(German, 1928–2005)
[Left: PP. 17, 52-53, Right: P. 17]

In Jünger's words, a true goldsmith is "a man who combines the two great human possibilities—Thought and Action—in one creative profession. He [is] a unified, unsplit person, and in this unity he finds the meaning and harmony of his existence."[8]

Pendant Necklace from the *Spiegel* Series (Munich, Germany), 2010; Silver, stainless steel, cord; 43.5 × 5 × 2.5 cm (17 1/8 in. × 1 15/16 in. × 1 in.); Promised gift

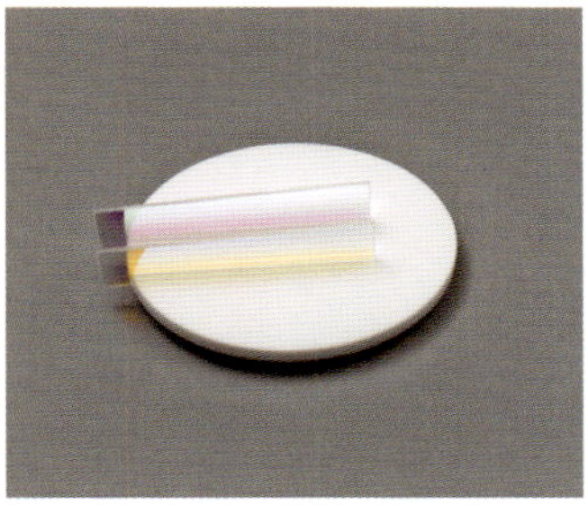

Brooch from the Palette Series (Munich, Germany), 2015; Dichroic mirror, Corian, silver; L x W x D: 9.5 × 6 × 2.2 cm (3 3/4 × 2 3/8 × 7/8 in.); Promised gift

Jiro Kamata
(Japanese, b. 1978)
[Left: PP. 23, 72, Right: PP. 116–117]

"**Spiegel Necklace** – I have been using old camera lenses in my work since 2008, fascinated with the idea of what they might have seen. This mirrored-lens pendant has a magical effect. If you look deeply you'll find a different world perhaps from long ago and discover your own image within. The mirror reflects reality, while the concave camera lens distorts the mirror's image."

"**Palette Brooch** is made with a dichroic mirror that reflects two colors. The wearer sees strong, colorful shadows on the white Corian base. The light is a living thing: it moves around, gets stronger or weaker, and changes color."

Pin Brooch from the Collection of different pin brooches Series (The Netherlands), 1992; Wood, textile, foam, acrylic paint, pins; 7 × 6.8 × 4.2 cm (2 3/4 × 2 11/16 × 1 5/8 in.); 2016-34-56

Beppe Kessler
(Dutch, b. 1952)
[P. 64]

"'Little treasures' is how I describe my pieces—miniature sculptures of age-old and contemporary materials, brazenly combined, not bound to the traditions of jewelry making. They express my feelings and thoughts about life. They invite touching and tell stories that are summarized in the titles."

Brooch from The Mind in the Hand Series (Israel), 2007; Silver embroidered with iron thread; 6.5 × 7.5 × 1 cm (2 9/16 × 2 15/16 × 3/8 in.); 2016-34-57

Brooch from the Immigrant Series (Israel), ca. 1990s; Recycled tin, painted fabric, nickel silver, stainless steel wire, elastic thread; 11.2 × 14 × 1.8 cm (4 7/16 × 5 1/2 × 11/16 in.); 2016-34-59

Esther Knobel
(Israeli, b. 1949, Poland)
[Left to Right: PP. 27, 26]

There's a trend in the US right now of calling jewelry 'small sculpture'—sort of to upgrade its status—but I don't buy it. I don't view my works as separate from the body, they always relate to the human proportion, the world or people. The context is human. Plus, the body is a good place to display them.[9]

Sensuous Thorn Bracelet from the Sculptural Bracelets Series (USA), 2011; Cast and oxidized silver, copper wire; 6.6 × 8.3 × 3.5 cm (2 5/8 × 3 1/4 × 1 3/8 in.); 2016-34-60

Shana Kroiz
(American, b. 1967)

"This cuff was created by carving a sensuous, flowing form that uses the wrist as its pedestal. I am influenced by a combination of primal tool and aquatic sea life. With the goal of also celebrating the female form and her sensuous nature. The bracelet was first carved in wax and then cast into sterling silver and fabricated to include copper tendril details and a hidden hinge and box clasp making it both sculptural and functional."

Necklace (Berlin, Germany), 2015; Clear and mirrored acrylic glass, pressed and layered flower petals and leaves, insects, silver, pigment; 32.5 x 15.7 x 1.1 cm (12 13/16 x 6 3/16 x 7/16 in); 2016-34-61

Necklace (Munich, Germany), 1987; Glass (oxidized windowpane fragments), gold, gold leaf; Promised gift

Daniel Kruger
(German, b. 1951, South Africa)
[Left: PP. 23, 76, Right: P. 65]

"The jewelry I make reflects both the semi-desert of southern Namibia where I grew up, a natural landscape in which humans have played a subordinate role and have left very few traces, and the European traditions in which I was socialized and educated. Thus my interest is in the natural and the artificial. My jewelry is intended to enhance the wearer, and wearing it should be a celebration. When it is not being worn, it is an artifact for reflection."

Pendant Necklace from the Fragments Series (Germany), 1986; Picture frame fragment, wood, steel; 35 × 26 × 3 cm (13 3/4 × 10 1/4 × 1 3/16 in.); 2016-34-62

Gold Makes You Blind (*Gold Macht Blind*) Bangle Bracelet (Munich, Germany), Designed: 1980, Executed: 2016; Black rubber over gold sphere; 8 × 8.5 × 1.2 cm (3 1/8 × 3 3/8 × 1/2 in.); 2016-34-63

Otto Künzli
(Swiss, b. 1948)
[Top Left and Right: PP. 34, 33; Bottom Left and Right: P. 34]

You could say this is conceptual, but it's not really. . . .I have so much humor and so much fun and I never call myself a conceptual artist. But it's kind of been established, so I stopped fighting it and said 'OK.'[10]

The Image (*Das Bild*) Brooch from *Das Bild* Series (Munich, Germany), 1981; Postcard in acrylic sleeve, brass, rubber band; 10.9 × 15.2 × 0.6 cm (4 5/16 in. × 6 in. × 1/4 in.); 2016-34-64

The Manhattan Piece Smoking Jewelry (Munich, Germany), 1987; Dannemann cigarillos box, brass, rubber, resin (Ureol), paper, linen (book); (Box Open): 1.5 × 8.7 × 22.2 cm (9/16 × 3 7/16 × 8 3/4 in.), (Box Closed): 1.5 × 8.7 × 11.3 cm (9/16 × 3 7/16 × 4 7/16 in.); 2016-34-65-a/d

Necklace from the Thunder I Series (Tallinn, Estonia), 2014; Black salt, oxidized silver, horn, wood, paint, green amethyst, hematite; 34.7 × 22 × 1.7 cm (13 11/16 × 8 11/16 × 11/16 in.); 2016-34-66

Kristiina Laurits
(Estonian, b. 1975)

"Each of the pieces of jewelry I make contains something that I didn't know before. Something elusive. Something that alters the boundaries of thoughts and actions and leads me to believe in things that are not known or understood by the light of day. By using a tactile material such as black salt, a mundane shirt collar turned into a sublime and spectacular neckpiece. The baroque ascent into the heavens can begin."

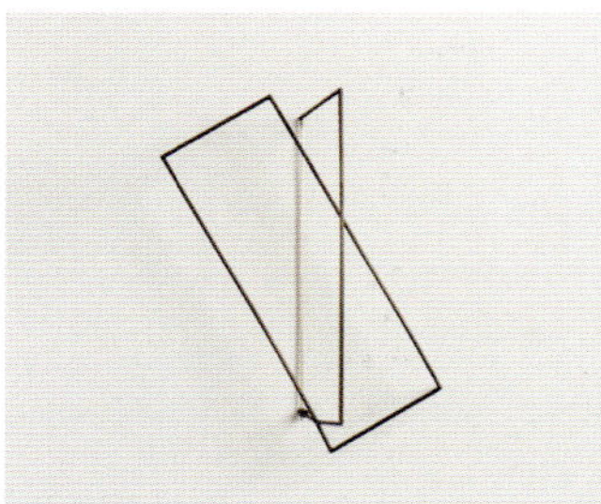

Brooch (Probably Lubbock, Texas, USA), ca. 1987; Steel, gold; 14.6 x 10.4 x 4.7 cm (5 3/4 × 4 1/8 × 1 7/8 in.); 2016-34-67

Leslie Leupp
(American, 1944–2011)

I wanted to use patterns and color; I was intrigued with angles and planes. Things were popping in the fields of metal and jewelry design: roller printing, photoetching, the use of titanium and aluminum, the marriage of metals, anodizing. Attitudes and philosophies were also changing.

People still want to put jewelry on and be very comfortable. They don't want anything to be disturbing; but that's not my work. If you put a piece of mine on, I want you to be disturbed . . . You are this thing now, since it changes your mental attitude as well as your physical posture.[11]

Untitled (15) Brooch (Westport, Connecticut, USA), 1992; Found objects (metal pocket watch case, leaf, glass beads, 19th-century engravings, vial, cork, sand), glass paste, metal; 7.6 × 5.8 × 2.5 cm (3 × 2 5/16 × 1 in.); 2016-34-68

Keith Lo Bue
(American, b. 1964)
[PP. 22, 71]

"What better vessel could I choose to house objects corraled from distant time than a case that would purport to tell it? Time, in this "verdigrised" case, is arrested. My process is crude, direct, and intuitive, while trying to create objects of careful detail and structure. This dichotomy keeps the creative impulse coursing through me, the thrill of making married with the spontaneity."

It's Getting So Dark Necklace (Estonia), 2015; Prehistoric shark's tooth, faceted citrine and fluorite, jet, hematite, silver, black coral; 46.1 × 14 × 2.6 cm (18 1/8 × 5 1/2 in. × 1 in.); Promised gift

Kadri Mälk
(Estonian, b. 1958)
[P. 68]

"During a performance of the Estonian composer Helena Tulve's chamber opera *It Is Getting So Dark*, which draws on the thousand-year-old texts in Sei Shōnagon's *The Pillow Book*, I envisioned a long, dark necklace. In the sketches for the piece, I sought to create a silent, soulful drama of "getting dark" through materials—a Mesozoic era fossilized shark's tooth, citrine, jet, and hematite—and the way I combined them."

Map of Venice Brooch, Study for the Periodical Research Series (Padua, Italy), 1999; Inlayed copper, silver, gold; 6.4 × 3.2 × 1 cm (2 1/2 × 1 1/4 × 3/8 in.); 2016-34-69

Stefano Marchetti
(Italian, b. 1970)
[P. 29]

"In 1998, I completed a piece of jewelry representing a map of Venice and a view of the land around it. That same year, I made another (shown here), wondering when research could be considered complete. In 2005, when I made still another piece inspired by the Venice map, it occurred to me that I could produce a piece about a given theme every ten years for the rest of my life. If I am lucky I will get to make three, four, or (not very realistically) five more pieces about this subject."

Due Respiri Necklace (Italy), 2005; Embossed gold sheets; 24 × 13.3 × 1.5 cm (9 7/16 × 5 1/4 × 9/16 in.); Promised gift

Eye Brooch (Italy), ca. 1995; Copper, stone; 2.7 x 5.7 x 1.5 cm (1 1/16 x 2 1/4 x 9/16 inches); 2016-34-70

Bruno Martinazzi
(Italian, b. 1923)
[Left: PP. 24, 80]

[I] presented reality in human body forms. The first series was the mouth-symbol of society's waste and greed that eventually devours itself. Next came the fist, representing encounters between forces, not necessarily of violence. After that, the hand-hand as creative, an instrument of knowledge and invention, meant to establish a relationship with others.[12]

Fulfillment Necklace (Philadelphia, Pennsylvania, USA), 2004; Carved and painted maple, gold-plated brass; 31 × 28 × 2.7 cm (12 3/16 × 11 × 1 1/16 in.); 2016-34-71-a,b

Bruce Metcalf
(American, b. 1949)
[P. 31]

"Jewelry, sex, and sensuality have been conjoined since the dawn of civilization. My proposal is that these ancient subjects—sex and sensuality—be repurposed for the twenty-first century. My goal is to make jewelry that is beautiful, sexy, and sometimes a little disturbing, so I offer clefts and blossoms, navels and seeds, antlers and leaves. Some of these images are reproductive in nature, others are abstractions. Indirect and suggestive, they create a potent tension with the veiled subject."

Corners Necklace from the Molten Jewelry Series (USA), 2006; Molten tin poured on commercial brass chain then silver-plated and oxidized; 27.5 × 15.3 × 0.5 cm (10 13/16 × 6 × 3/16 in.); Promised gift

Myra Mimlitsch-Gray
(American, b. 1962)
[P. 123]

"In this series, Molten Jewelry, I explored the conditions of molten metal and design by chance, framing the experiments within the construct of fashion jewelry. I sloshed molten tin onto chain and tried to distance myself from the controlled circumstances that define the goldsmith's practice. The use of commercial chain and gold-/silver-plating techniques is a transparent attempt to make precious what had been an accident—a spill. Plating sits on the surface of the free form like applied make-up: it seeks to mask that which we know to be less than pristine—to be imperfect."

Tourmaline Brooch II (USA), 1980; Silver, polished tourmalinated quartz, ivory; H x W x D: 5.8 × 5.4 × 1.4 cm (2 5/16 × 2 1/8 × 9/16 in.); 2016-34-73

Eleanor Moty
(American, b. 1945)
[PP. 13, 45]

"For me, designing a brooch begins with a unique stone that has striking graphic imagery. For Tourmaline Brooch II, I selected a slice of quartz crystal with black rod-like inclusions of tourmaline crystals that evoke the image of reeds emerging from ice on a frozen pond. To emphasize this image, I polished the quartz to a frosted, or matte, finish and enhanced the composition with the dynamic black slash of a natural tourmaline crystal. The unobtrusive silver setting allows the stone and complementary elements to be the focus."

Brooch (Tokyo, Japan), 2015; Folded linen paper, nylon thread, gold wire, silver; 11.3 × 8 × 4.1 cm (4 7/16 × 3 1/8 × 1 5/8 in.); 2016-34-74

Kazumi Nagano
(Japanese, b. 1946)
[PP. 31, 120]

"The concept for my jewelry is "calm and beautiful" because I think that the essence of Japanese culture is "calm and beautiful." Origami, the traditional Japanese art of paper folding, has been my inspiration for folding handmade paper into 3-D jewelry. I don't begin by working out the design on paper; I make the shape with my hands according to an image in my mind. It is a satisfactory means of production that only requires my fingers."

Crazy Glasses Necklace (The Netherlands), 2008; Silver, fur, snakeskin; 45 × 15 × 2.5 cm (17 11/16 in. × 5 7/8 in. × 1 in.); 2016-34-75

Necklace from the Fred Pendant Series (The Netherlands), 2003; Fly and pearl in cast acrylic resin, cord; 4 x 2.5 x 1.2 cm (1 9/16 x 1 x 1/2 in.); 2016-34-76

Brooch from The Droog Collection Mercedes Benz Brooches Series (The Netherlands), 2003; Fragment cut from painted steel body of a Mercedes Benz; 2.8 × 13.6 × 1.5 cm (1 1/8 × 5 3/8 × 9/16 in.); 2016-34-77

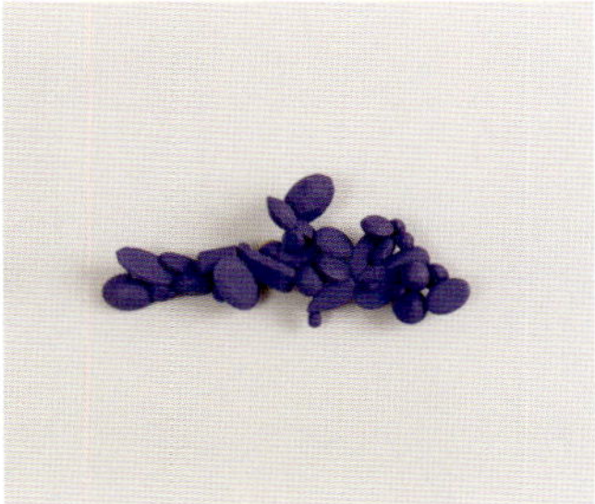

Mom Brooch from the Haunted by 36 Women Series (The Netherlands), 2009; 3D-printed and dyed nylon; 6 × 13 × 1.6 cm (2 3/8 × 5 1/8 × 5/8 in.); 2016-34-78

Ted Noten
(Dutch, b. 1956)
[Top Left/Right, Bottom Left: PP. 34,35, 128]

"**Crazy Glasses Necklace** – I make jewelry for a variety of different reasons. Crazy Glasses was a challenge to the wearer to put the silver-plated glasses on his nose and enjoy the world."

"**Fred Pendant Necklace** – This Fred pendant necklace and similar pieces were an attempt to make affordable democratic jewelry."

"**Mercedes Benz Brooch** – Fragments cut from the bright red body of a Mercedes—were made to give more than just a privileged few the fun of owning an internationally recognized symbol of success and social prestige."

"**Mom Brooch** – This brooch is inspired by Japanese artist Katsushika Hokusai's 36 Views of Mount Fuji. The series depicts 36 archetypal views of women to capture these different feminine types in sculpture. Each unique sculpture is made from found objects, then 3D-scanned, and scaled down versions are 3D-printed in quantity, as jewelry. Transformation from one-of-a-kind artwork to mass produced object is like the work of fashion designers, whose haute couture collections become the basis for affordable ready-to-wear lines, blending concepts of art and design."

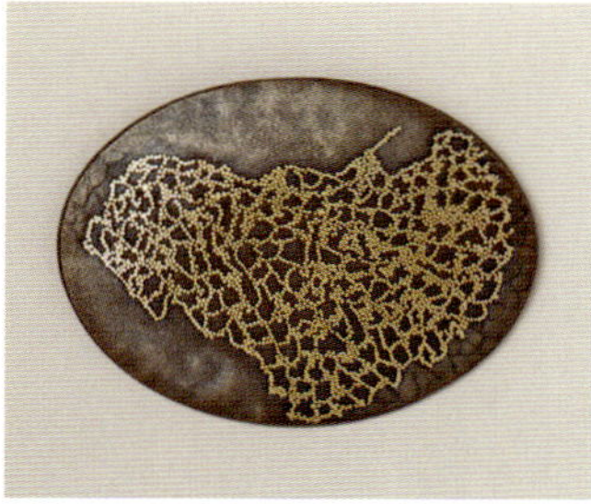

Sea Fan Brooch from the Up from the Deep Series (Salida, Colorado, USA), 1992; Fabricated, roller-printed, and granulated silver and gold; 4.5 × 6.5 × 0.5 cm (1 3/4 × 2 9/16 × 3/16 in.); 2016-34-79

Harold O'Connor
(American, b. 1941)

"The title of the piece comes from the roller printing under metal resulting in the creation of an image of the fan on the metal sheets. First the silver sheet was granulated (fusing small metal balls to surface); then this was rolled flat. Next was to place gold balls on the surface and fire them in place. The piece was rolled again so all the balls are flat. The final step was to oxidize the brooch."

Bracelet and Brooch (Tokyo, Japan), 2005, 2010; Rolled, pasted, and cut corrugated cardboard, silver; (Brooch): 8.9 × 10.2 × 9.2 cm (3 1/2 × 4 × 3 5/8 in.), (bracelet): 8 × 13.5 × 8.7 cm (3 1/8 × 5 5/16 × 3 7/16 in.); 2016-34-80-a,b

Ritsuko Ogura
(Japanese, b. 1951)
[P. 31]

"I use cardboard to make jewelry because it is a cheap, common factory-made material. Generally it is destined to be thrown away, but by my hand it is transformed into beautiful jewelry. First I cut the cardboard to the proper length then I paint both sides of the cardboard. After the paint has dried, I apply paste and roll the sheet into a log. When the paste is dry, I cut the cardboard into the final piece."

Brooch (Czech Republic), ca. 1990; Designed by Pavel Opočenský (Czech, b. 1954); ColorCore Formica, metal; 8.9 × 8.9 × 0.6 cm (3 1/2 × 3 1/2 × 1/4 in.); 2016-34-81

Pavel Opočenský
(Czech, b. 1954)

Cono Brooch (Padua, Italy), 2015; Stoneware (gres ceramic), gold with niello (alloy of silver, copper, and lead sulfides); 7.5 × 6.5 × 1.5 cm (2 15/16 × 2 9/16 × 9/16 in.); 2016-34-9

Renzo Pasquale
(Italian, b. 1947)
[PP. 28, 105]

"I love to create wearable jewelry in which the beauty is in the simplicity of the lines and the exploration of form. Normally my jewels are made of hard stone such as lapis lazuli, agate, chrysoprase, quartz, rock crystal, and jasper, and are placed in metal geometric structures. In this brooch, I inserted a new material—stoneware—to create a plastic effect between the black of the niello and that of the stoneware."

Brooch (Italy), ca. 1985; Red gold, silver, copper, nickel silver; 8.1 × 8.8 × 2.4 cm (3 3/16 × 3 7/16 × 15/16 in.); 2016-34-82

Francesco Pavan
(Italian, b. 1937)
[PP. 28, 104]

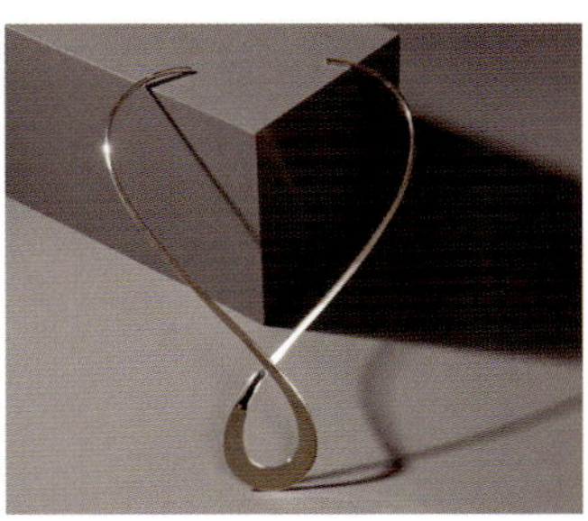

Necklace (USA), ca. 1975; Silver; 18.5 × 13.3 × 1.6 cm (7 5/16 × 5 1/4 × 5/8 in.); 2016-34-83

Ronald Hayes Pearson
(American, 1924–1996)
[P. 13]

I believe that designing must be a continuing, consuming, and lifelong process, one that requires considerable self-discipline and constant practice.[13]

Gaetano Pesce
(Italian, b. 1939)
[Left: P. 32]

"I have been making resin invitations for my exhibitions for over forty years. Each is handmade and thus a small piece of art in itself, part of the exhibition. It's an invitation you cannot throw away. The jewelry is part of a series of experiments that I have been conducting in my spare time on Saturdays and Sundays for the past eight or nine years."

Bracelet (New York, New York, USA), 2009; Polyurethane resin; 7.2 × 11 cm (2 13/16 × 4 5/16 in.); 2016-34-84

One Man Show at Material Connection Invitation/Bracelet (New York, New York, USA), 1997; Poured and imprinted polyurethane resin; L x W x D: 22 × 7.5 × 1.3 cm (8 11/16 × 2 15/16 × 1/2 in.); 2016-34-85

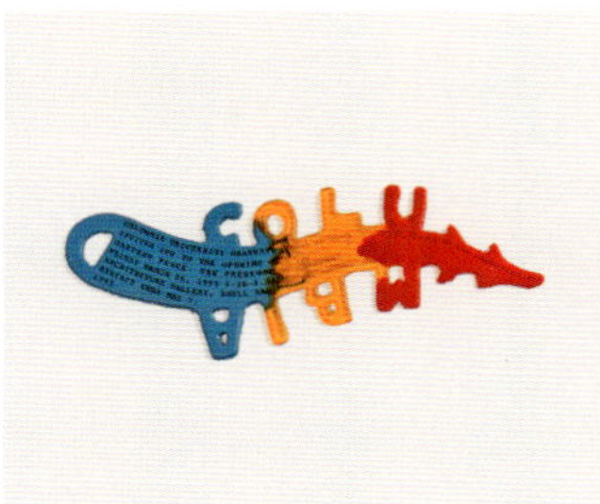

Columbia University Exhibition "The Presence of Objects" Invitation/ Bracelet (New York, New York, USA), 1999; Polyurethane resin; 8.5 × 24 × 0.3 cm (3 3/8 × 9 7/16 × 1/8 in.); 2016-34-86

Allouche Gallery Exhibition "One of a Kind Iconic Works" Invitation (New York, New York, USA), 2015; Polyurethane resin; 8 × 26.2 × 0.3 cm (3 1/8 × 10 5/16 × 1/8 in.); 2016-34-87

Collective Design Fair Invitation (New York, New York, USA), 2013; Polyurethane resin; 13 × 34.8 × 0.5 cm (5 1/8 × 13 11/16 × 3/16 in.); 2016-34-88

Fish Design Invitation, (New York, New York, USA), 2004; Polyurethane resin; 13 × 21.8 × 0.7 cm (5 1/8 × 8 9/16 × 1/4 in.); 2016-34-89

Necklace from the Lapis Series (Amsterdam, The Netherlands), 1997; Ground jade mixed and cast with acrylic resin, gold; 17.3 × 12.5 × 7 cm (6 13/16 × 4 15/16 × 2 3/4 in.); 2016-34-90

Ruudt Peters
(Dutch, b. 1950)
[PP. 21, 69]

The mysterious cause for this collection was a quote taken from an old alchemical text: 'Grind the stone to a very fine powder and put it into the sharpest vinegar, and it will at once be dissolved into the philosophical water.' Peters started creating his own stones by grinding precious minerals and mixing the grit with liquid acrylic and then pouring this material into moulds [sic] taken from other minerals.[14]

Brooch from the Canvas Series (Munich, Germany), 2014; Painted canvas on wood, applied tin, silver, iron; 10 × 6.2 × 2.8 cm (3 15/16 × 2 7/16 × 1 1/8 in.); 2016-34-91

Karen Pontoppidan
(Danish, b. 1968)
[P. 33]

In the group Canvas, my intention was to use my goldsmithing background as a lens for decision-making. After I finished the Canvas brooches, I wondered to what degree, I have given my inner goldsmith precedence over my artistic intentions. Although I love the making process, as an artist I am convinced that the making in itself cannot and should not be the aim of my work. I therefore decided to continue examining the material of canvas in jewelry, but with a process that excluded me from the manufacturing.[15]

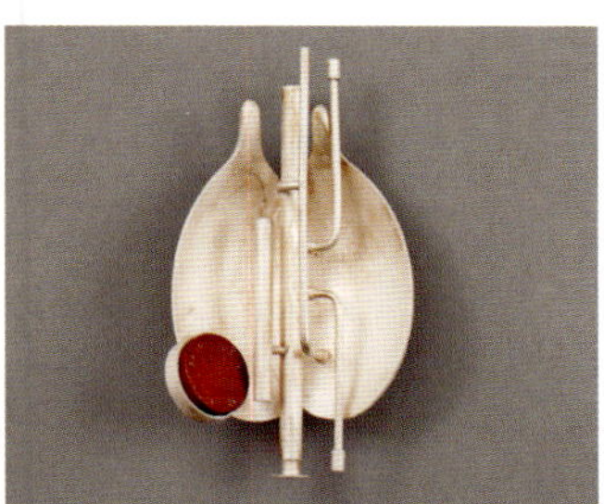

Brooch from the Continuum Series (Amsterdam, The Netherlands), 2007; Silver, sealing wax; 9 × 5.5 × 2.6 cm (3 9/16 in. × 2 3/16 in. × 1 in.); 2016-34-92

Katja Prins
(Dutch, b. 1970)
[PP. 24, 82]

"Through my work I tell stories about the body as an object of manipulation, an instrument, and a machine. I also address topics such as plastic surgery, medical biology, gene/stem cell technology, implants, prosthetics, and how machinery, robotica, industry, and architecture are related to us. My hope is that people will discover their own stories through my work."

Flyer Necklace (Halle, Germany), 2010; Cut and drilled elm wood, cord; 42 × 26 × 5.2 cm (16 9/16 × 10 1/4 × 2 1/16 in.); Promised gift

Dorothea Prühl
(German, b. 1937)
[PP. 30, 118]

"Apart from the personal point of view, there is hardly anything new to invent. Everything was in some way already. In this sense, my work is similar to a string of pearls, but each necklace that I make has a theme and is the result of my search for a form that moves me. The final form evolves out of considerations concerning function and the properties of the wood itself."

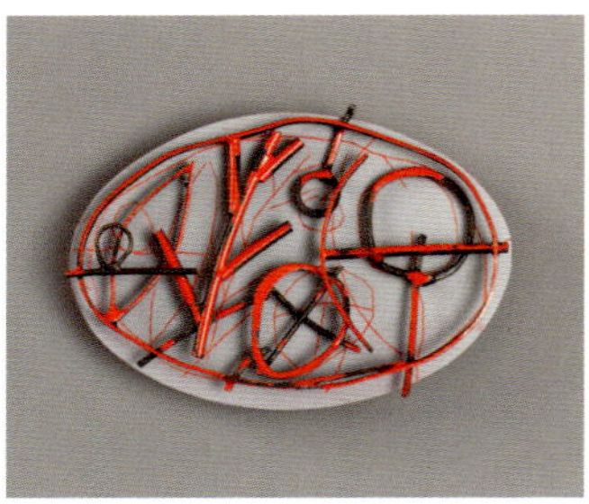

Brooch No. 953 from the Walled Garden Series (Barcelona, Spain), 2004; Painted wood, plastic, silver, painted acrylic; 5 × 7.1 × 1.8 cm (1 15/16 × 2 13/16 × 11/16 in.); 2016-34-93

Ramón Puig Cuyàs
(Spanish, b. 1953)
[PP. 21, 66–67]

"These pieces are an expression of my desire to use color without inhibition, to create pieces without pretensions. They are a very personal attempt at an intimate experience of freedom and to satisfy a deep need to feel alive. Walled Gardens alludes to gardens that we imagine or that we catch a glimpse of through iron gates or over high walls. They awaken in us the desire to transgress forbidden boundaries and discover the universe within."

Three Cone Necklace from the Wedgwood and Wendy Ramshaw Collection (London, England, United Kingdom), 1982; Gold, nickel alloy, unglazed stoneware (jasperware); 39.5 × 17.2 × 2.5 cm (15 9/16 × 6 3/4 × 1 in.); 2016-34-94

Wendy Ramshaw
(British, b. 1939)
[PP. 18, 54]

"Most of the pieces in my collaboration with Wedgwood were made with their famous jasper clay, a dense white vitrified stone body having properties much the same as porcelain. I made several hundred sketches of pieces but unexpectedly most of the units I decided to use took the form of beads—a fundamental and basic element in jewelry used by jewelers around the world."

Tropical Punch Necklace (Hamburg, Germany), 2006; Glass, crystal, resin, metal and plastic beads, ribbon, thread, gold; 41 ×11 × 3.7 cm (16 1/8 × 4 5/16 × 1 7/16 in.); 2016-34-95

Axel Russmeyer
(German, b. 1964)
[P. 88]

"My signature technique and its limitations help me to focus almost purely on color and texture and the juxtaposition and combination of these design elements. I work with needle and thread, using beads of all colors, sizes, textures, ages, and materials. While making the beaded beads can be quite time consuming, making a necklace like this is a rather quick, playful process. This necklace is created with twenty-nine beaded beads."

Necklace (Amsterdam, The Netherlands), 2006; Antique textile, rubber, onyx, nylon, zinc; 43.5 × 9.5 × 4.3 cm (17 1/8 × 3 3/4 × 1 11/16 in.); Promised gift

Lucy Sarneel
(Dutch, b. 1961)
[P. 20]

"Material and idea are equally merged in my working process. Either I have a specific idea in mind that drives me to search for the appropriate materialization or a material itself instigates thoughts and associations that evolve into a piece. The textile in this necklace would have been worn during light mourning in the village of Marken, near Amsterdam. The onyx beads and zinc "tears" also refer to mourning and grief."

Necklace (USA), 2000s; Glass beads, thread (Peyote-stitch technique); 34.2 x 24 x 1.5 cm (13 7/16 x 9 7/16 x 9/16 in.); Promised gift

Joyce Scott
(American, b. 1948)
[PP. 26, 94]

"My approach is to confound the viewer and myself with my ability to spin tales from tiny orbs of glass. Employing the Peyote Stitch as the basic formula allows me to create using light and structure, generally without an armature. This blue woman conveys emotion/motion, the human body expressed as any artist in any medium would, except in beads. Elevating and reexamining this ancient technique assists in propelling my abilities beyond those usually found in this art form. I am a 'Reinventress.'"

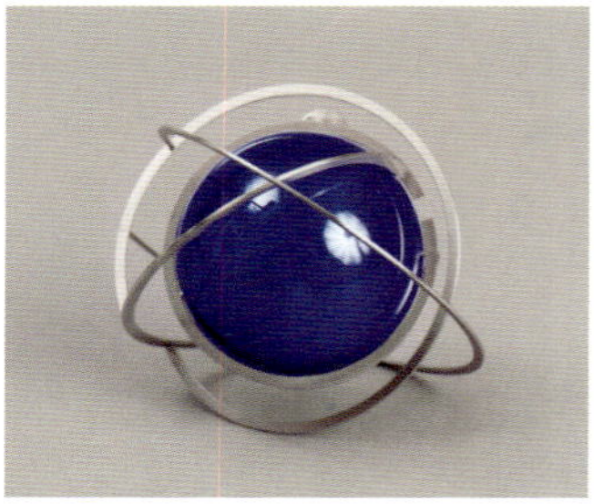

Brooch from the Twisted Circles Series (Brno, Czech Republic), 2001; Cold-connected, riveted stainless steel and acrylic; 7 × 8 × 7.5 cm (2 3/4 × 3 1/8 × 2 15/16 in.); 2016-34-96

Jiří Šibor
(Czech, b. 1966)
[P. 115]

"In my Twisted Circles series, I explore the possibilities of discontinuous circles in space. This time-intensive process involves coupling ideas with the properties of the materials used. Intentionally open-ended, the concept gives accident a chance, resulting in structures difficult to define in geometric terms. The works were created out of the essence of the circle, which can be perceived as a symbol of infinity. Its transmutation and fixation in three-dimensional form offers a subtle clue as to the universe's complexity."

Necklace (The Hague, The Netherlands), 2010; Enameled steel, steel, silver, sawn, embossed, enameled, mounted; 32.5 × 23 × 3.2 cm (12 13/16 × 9 1/16 × 1 1/4 in.); 2016-34-97

Vera Siemund
(German, b. 1971)
[P. 22]

"When I made this necklace, I had begun to shake off some of the nineteenth-century ornamentation of my earlier work in search of simpler shapes more characteristic of the 1960s and '70s. The sharp contrast of black and white in the portraits of the femmes fatales fascinated me and reminded me of the op art or psychedelic art of the time. Still, I didn't choose colorful plastic. I chose a solid, ageless, dark material, and a simple contrast of black and white."

Necklace (USA), 1973; Bent silver wire, sheet silver, polished moonstone; 19.5 × 15.4 × 2.2 cm (7 11/16 × 6 1/16 × 7/8 in.); Promised gift

Olaf Skoogfors
(American, b. Sweden, 1930–1975)
[PP. 13, 47]

Jewelry offers me the opportunity to control artistic expression from a concept to realization and provides me with the human body as a gallery.[16]

Brooch from the Mirror Brooches Series (Gamischdorf, Austria), 2001; 14 × 8.5 × 9.4 cm (5 1/2 × 3 3/8 × 3 11/16 in.); Promised gift

Peter Skubic
(Austrian, b. Serbia, 1935)
[PP. 30, 111]

"Since 1999, I have worked on a series of pieces with mirrors in them. Mirrors are invisible. You only see the reflection of the surroundings. I used reflective stainless steel in this brooch, and I see the piece as an architectural model and as sculpture. About making: you never ask a painter how he mixed his colors; it is not important how I made this. I like the form of my jewelry to be hard, not lovely; good but not nice; and not made from a valuable material."

Hot Bed Brooch from the Re: Pair and Imperfection Series (Chicago, Illinois, USA), 2006; Silver, carved wood fragment (figure), coral (brooch); 11.2 × 6.4 × 2.5 cm (4 7/16 in. × 2 1/2 in. × 1 in.); 2016-34-72-a,b

Reliquary of My Own Making Necklace (USA), 2008; Photo transparencies, mica, silver; 30.2 × 26 × 1.8 cm (11 7/8 × 10 1/4 × 11/16 in.); 2016-34-98

Signature Piece Necklace (USA), 2005; Mass-produced metal-rimmed key tags, ink; 35.6 × 20.3 × 2.5 cm (14 × 8 × 1 in.); 2016-34-99

Ojo de Agua Necklace (USA and Oaxaca, Mexico), 2005; Hand-made paper; 1.2 × 32 cm (1/2 × 12 5/8 in.); 2016-34-100

Kiff Slemmons
(American, b. 1944)
[Top Left and Right: P. 27]

"Reliquary of My Own Making is a piece that depicts the making of the necklace itself in photographs. This is a single, stand-alone piece, whereas for many years most of my work has been made up of pieces exploring a set of ideas, scale, and material as metaphor. For the most part, I don't work with the masterpiece idea—the perfectly contained piece—the kind of piece that usually represents artists in museums. I like pieces that work together, like jazz, in an exhibition or performance.

For the exhibition *Re:Pair and Imperfection*, I called on artists whose work I admire to send me a fragment of their work that had been abandoned or stalled. The carved wood fragment in Hot Bed was sent to me by Bruce Metcalf. I decided not to disturb the beautifully carved fragment itself and fabricated a silver "nest" with coral flames for its resting place, with the idea that this juxtaposition would evoke a hotbed of ideas."

(Work continues on page 164.)

Mitla Necklace (USA and Oaxaca, Mexico), 2012; Hand-made paper; 3.2 × 26 cm (1 1/4 × 10 1/4 in.); 2016-34-101

Art Smith
(American, b. Cuba, 1917–1982)
[Top Left: PP. 11, 40]

A piece of jewelry is in a sense an object that is not complete in itself. Jewelry is a 'what is it?' until you relate it to the body. The body is a component in design just as air and space are. Like line, form, and color, the body is a material to work with. It is one of the basic inspirations in creating form.[17]

Modernette Cuff Bracelet (New York, New York, USA), Designed 1948, this example probably after 1948; Bent and flattened copper wire, bent and patinated sheet brass; 6.4 × 6 × 6 cm (2 1/2 × 2 3/8 × 2 3/8 in.); 2016-34-102

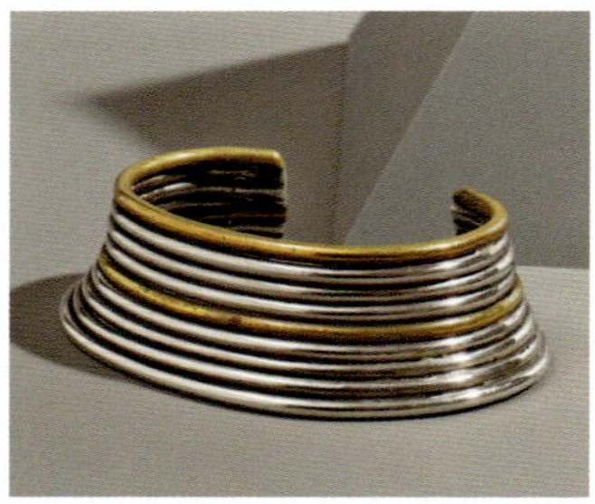

Bracelet (New York, New York, USA), ca. 1955, Bent brass and silver wire; 5.5 × 7.2 × 2.5 cm (2 3/16 × 2 13/16 × 1 in.); 2016-34-103

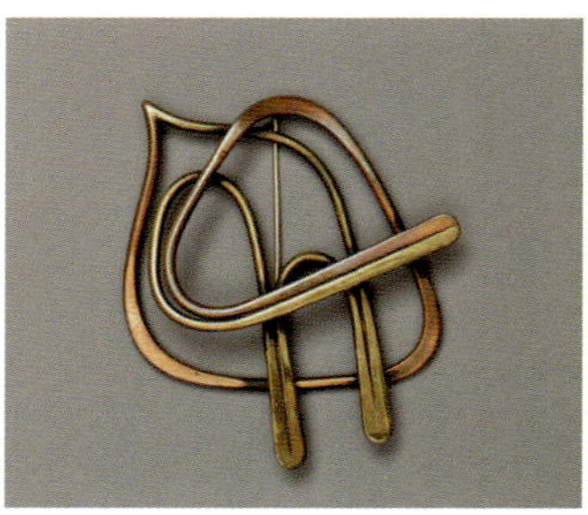

Angular Brooch (New York, New York, USA), Designed 1949, this example probably after 1949; Bent and flattened brass and copper wire; 8.5 × 8.7 × 1.5 cm (3 7/8 × 3 1/4 × 1/4 in.); 2016-34-104

Necklace (USA), 1989; Dominoes, silver, leather cord; 28.5 × 20.5 × 1.3 cm (11 1/4 × 8 1/16 × 1/2 in.); 2016-34-105

Ramona Solberg
(American, 1921–2005)
[PP. 15, 49]

I start with the object. I start with the domino or the bead or the scraper or whatever. And this is, I think, why. . . my work, as I look at it—my little table full of odds and ends—they all look quite different. But it's because the object starts me off, and it starts me off in a direction. And, of course, all I want to do is make something to hang around my neck.

Now, I have a tendency to sometimes overdo. I get carried away. Like in my house I have, you know, too many things. But, you know, I love it all and I just want to put it down.[18]

Brooch (Germany), 2005; Ferrotype (or "Tintype"), silver, silver wire, rubies, marcasite; 8.9 × 6 × 0.6 cm (3 1/2 × 2 3/8 × 1/4 in.); 2016-34-106

Bettina Speckner
(German, b. 1962)
[PP. 22, 70]

"I never work with the intention of decorating things or making them look prettier. I try to discover the soul of an object or the essence of a photograph and try to shape something new that will appeal to me and other people, something that goes far beyond the optical appearance. My pieces don't talk about situations. They give access to stories. But who owns the stories? We, the beholders or the piece itself?"

Two Bracelets from the Aluminum Bracelets Series (Brooklyn, New York, USA), 1988 (a), 1990 (b); Etched aluminum; (a) 16.5 × 0.3 cm (6 1/2 × 1/8 in.), (b) 19 × 0.3 cm (7 1/2 × 1/8 in.); 2016-34-107-a,b

Lisa Spiros
(American, b. 1959)

"My primary choice of material is metal for its fluid response to shape, association with endurance, and the multiple surface possibilities. Using what could be called utilitarian metal is complementary to the primary design emphasis. In the integration of materials, technical skill, and what I call abstract, intuitive know how, I find both inspiration and resolution."

Necklace from the Kalandia Checkpoint Series (Herzliya, Israel), 2007; Crushed aluminum soda cans, zircons; 5.5 × 11 × 0.9 cm (2 3/16 × 4 5/16 × 3/8 in.); 2016-34-108

Deganit Stern Schocken
(Israeli, b. 1947)
[PP. 26, 97]

"Visiting the Kalandia military checkpoint, I collected crushed soft-drink cans with Arabic writing that had been smashed by army vehicles and were thrown by the roadside as garbage. In 2007, I turned these smashed cans into precious pendants by adding found precious stones or zircons. I titled the series Kalandia Checkpoint. This was my way of protesting against military checkpoints and the way Palestinians are treated by the Israeli army."

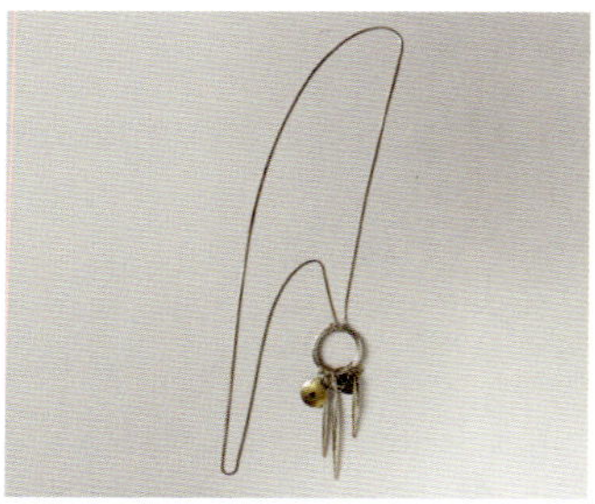

Reflections of St. Mary's Necklace (El Paso, Texas, USA), 1994; Sterling silver, gold, carved slate; 73 × 8 × 1 cm (28 3/4 × 3 1/8 × 3/8 in.); 2016-34-109

Rachelle Thiewes
(American, b. 1952)

"My jewelry is designed to engage and challenge the wearer. Through the jewelry's kinetic properties, the wearer's movement triggers sounds and rhythms and sets off an ever-changing display of visual chaos. The high Chihuahuan desert of West Texas, which pushes boldly, dramatically, aggressively, and seductively up to the barren mountains, has played a pivotal role in shaping the way I approach my jewelry. My exploration of rhythm and sound is drawn from my interest in music."

Necklace from the Clockwork Love Wings Gold Series (Amsterdam, The Netherlands), 2009; Chemically-etched, gold-plated stainless steel; 49 × 9.4 × 1.5 cm (19 5/16 × 3 11/16 × 9/16 in.); 2016-34-111-a/d

Frank Tjepkema
(Dutch, b. 1970)

"The combination of simplicity and complexity is a theme that fascinates me. Most of my jewelry could not be designed without the computer, yet the result often has a hand-made quality. When people look at this pendant they may think that it consists of hundreds of tiny parts, whereas it consists of only five parts arranged in layers, creating the illusion of complexity. Creating depth through layering has become an important part of my work in many different projects and on different scales."

Manufactured by Georg Jensen Sølvsmedie; Model No. 203A Bangle Bracelet (Copenhagen, Denmark), 1968; Sterling silver, rutilated smoky quartz; 6.2 × 6 × 5.5 cm (2 7/16 × 2 3/8 × 2 3/16 in.); 2016-34-112

Vivianna Torun Bülow-Hübe
(Swedish, 1927–2004)
[PP. 18, 46]

It should be possible to hang up the washing while wearing my jewellery! I wanted it to be natural, anatomical: adapted to the movements of the human body, to slide up and down, back and forth on the arm. At that time, I also created my so-called body sculptures, the asymmetrically "climbing" necklaces for festive occasions.[19]

Whorl Pendant Neckpiece from the Embodiment Series (High Falls, New York, USA), 2010; Carved cow and ox bone, snake vertebrae, resin, plastic (found objects), diamonds, gold, silver; 28.5 x 17 x 3.4 cm; (11 ¼ x 6 11/16 x 15/16 in.); Promised gift

Jennifer Trask
(American, b. 1970)
[PP. 23, 77]

"The question while working on the series was "What is written in our bones?" What desires, ideals, and motivations do we carry silently? My approach was to literally inlay metals and minerals into flat sections of bone—as if viewing electron microscope images. The wearable object became a matrix, as if an extension, and external appendage of the wearer's own bones. Combining found materials, delicately carved florals with rough fragments of skull, teeth, or antler formed an uneasy ornamental idiom."

Object with Ring/Grey Heron Airplane Ring (Amsterdam, The Netherlands), 2006; Plastic heron, gold, glass beads, marcasite; textile; 5 x 13 x 7.5 cm (2 3/4 × 4 1/4 × 3 in.); 2016-34-113-a/c

Felieke van der Leest
(Dutch, b. 1968)
[P. 89]

"I combine mass-produced miniature toy animals with crocheted textiles, metalwork—usually gold or silver—and needlework to make my jewelry. I start each piece with an idea of what I want to do with the animal, but the idea can change a lot during the working process. The stories people see in the work are all different, and I like that. They see things I didn't see myself."

Bracelet (The Netherlands), ca. 1980; PVC, paper; 7.8 x 6.1 cm. (3 1/16 x 2 3/8 in.); 2016-34-114

Emmy van Leersum
(Dutch, 1930–1984)
[PP. 16, 51]

I'm not sure that my work really has that much to do with jewellery. It's more to do with people, with shapes; getting away from simply buying gold. That tradition has never appealed to me. I think you should have a reason for wearing something.[20]

Necklace from the Spaces Series (Menomonie, Wisconsin, USA), 2015; Steel, acrylic paint, polyester cord, thread; techniques: template-making, drilling, painting, stitching, forming; 54 × 12.4 × 2.7 cm (21 1/4 × 4 7/8 × 1 1/16 in.); Promised gift

Aric Verrastro
(American, b. 1985)

"Recently, I was displaced from the city I lived in, which has left an emptiness in my life. Creating jewelry allows me to reflect on city living. The modular, architectural steel forms in this necklace serve as allegorical representations of a thriving, vibrant environment. The thread acts as a metaphorical timeline for an individual's pathway meandering along the busy streets. Just as the body completes jewelry, people give life to architectural spaces, expressing the connection I feel toward urban living."

Brooch from the Sasso Series (Milan and Rome, Italy), 2000; Electroformed copper, silver, mixed media, magnets (clasp); 7.6 × 7 × 4.4 cm (3 in. × 2 3/4 in. × 1 3/4 in.); 2016-34-115

Giorgio Vigna
(Italian, b. 1955)

"I am an artist who creates natural forms capable of manifesting primary and primordial aspects at the boundary between reality and imagination, where earth, water, fire, and wind combine along with the natural and the artificial, the poor and the precious. I operate on the border between what is and what appears to be. This "stone" appears to be heavy, but in reality it is light and can be worn through the use of an inner and outer magnet."

NOTES

1 http://www.babetto.com/index2_en.htm.

2 https://www.youtube.com/watch?v=dc8fuEggeuA.

3 Based on Maria Elenskaya's article "Kunst ist eine behauptung," at current-obsession.com: http://www.current-obsession.com/manfred-bischoff/.

4 Adapted from Renee C. Hoogland's introduction in *Iris Eichenberg: Weiss*, Galerie Louise Smit: Amsterdam, The Netherlands, 2005].

5 Adapted from Renee C. Hoogland's introduction in *Iris Eichenberg: Weiss*, Galerie Louise Smit: Amsterdam, The Netherlands, 2005.

6 http://www.aaa.si.edu/collections/interviews/oral-history-interview-claire-falkenstein-12659.

7 Adapted from Waard Schrijver's statement for the Dolomitensagen Series exhibition at Galerie Rob Koudijs, Amsterdam, The Netherlands, September 1–October 6, 2007. http://www.galerierobkoudijs.nl/en/exhibitions/archive/dolomieten-sagen?page=17.

8 Hermann Jünger, 1979, as quoted in "A Goldsmith's World," *Art Aurea* 1 (1989): 58.

9 From Rachel Neiman's article *Israel's Esther Knobel goes beyond fashion*, July 13, 2008, 10:17 a.m. https://www.israel21c.org/israels-esther-knobel-goes-beyond-fashion/.

10 http://www.japantimes.co.jp/culture/2015/12/01/arts/otto-kunzlis-real-statement-jewelry/#.WVGOgnErLIU.

11 From quote in Elizabeth Skidmore Sasser's article, "Leslie Leupp: Exploring the Possibilities" in *Metalsmith Magazine*, Summer, 1987. Derived from: https://www.ganoksin.com/article/leslie-leupp-exploring-possibilities/.

12 As quoted in *Autobiography of Bruno Martinazzi, Goldsmith and Sculptor, Professor at the "Academia di Belle Arte di Torino", Italy,* Goldsmiths' Journal, Vol. V, Number 4, August, 1979, p. 37.

13 As quoted in Daniel Rhode's article, "Form in Silver By Ronald Pearson," *Craft Horizons*, (November/December 1960), p. 21. Derived from: http://digital.craftcouncil.org/digital/collection/p15785coll2/id/6334/rec/1.

14 Liesbeth den Besten, "Ruudt Peters: My Jewelry is My Laboratory," *Metalsmith Magazine*, Vol. 28, Issue 1, 2008, p. 45.

15 Benjamin Lignel, *Interview: In Conversation with Karen Pontoppidan*. Art Jewelry Forum, 10/19/2016. https://artjewelryforum.org/in-conversation-with-karen-pontoppidan.

16 As quoted in *Olaf Skoogfors: 20th-Century Goldsmith, 1930–1975* (Philadelphia: Philadelphia College of Art, 1979), p. 42.

17 *Art Smith Jewelry* (exhibition brochure), American Crafts Council, Museum of Contemporary Crafts, 1969, pp. 1-6, quoted in *From the Village to Vogue: The Modernist Jewelry of Art Smith*, Barry Harwood, Brooklyn Museum, 2008, pp. 2 and 5.

18 Oral history interview with Ramona Solberg, March 23, 2001: https://www.aaa.si.edu/collections/interviews/oral-history-interview-ramona-solberg-12835.

19 Ann Westin, *Torun: Conversation With Vivianna Torun Bülow-Hübe*, Stockholm, Sweden: Carlsson, 1993, p. 88.

20 As quoted in *Zero Karat: The Donna Schneier Gift to the American Craft Museum* (New York, N.Y.: American Craft Museum, 2002), p. 126.

21 As quoted in Jan Conradi, *Lella and Massimo Vignelli, Two Lives, One Vision* (Rochester, N.Y.: Rochester Institute of Technology Press, 2014), p. 77.

Gallery of Jewelry Drawings and Works on Paper Captions

All credit lines The Susan Grant Lewin Collection, Cooper Hewitt, Smithsonian Design Museum, unless otherwise noted. All photos by Matt Flynn © Smithsonian Institution

P. 92: Print, The Mind in the Hand (Israel); 2006; Etching from embossed aluminum plate on white wove paper, perforated and stitched with iron thread; 25.4 × 28.3 cm (10 × 11 1/8 in.); 2016-34-58

P. 106: Drawing, Designs for a Brooch (Padua, Italy), 2002; Graziano Visintin (Italian, b. 1954); Graphite, black and red color pencil, brush and gold paint on cream wove paper mounted on white wove paper; 9.5 × 13 cm (3 3/4 × 5 1/8 in.)

P. 109: Drawings, Designs for Roofs Brooch (Padua, Italy), 2002: Annamaria Zanella (Italian, b. 1966); Pen and black ink, brush and watercolor, graphite on cream wove paper; each: 29.7 × 21 cm (11 11/16 × 8 1/4 in.); 2016-34-121/123

P. 124: Drawing, Postpriori II Brooch (High Falls, New York, USA), 2009: Jamie Bennett (American, b. 1948); Brush and watercolor, pen and ink, graphite on white wove paper; 22.9 × 33 cm (9 × 13 in.); 22.9 × 30.5 cm (9 × 12 in.); Gift of Jamie Bennett, 2017-29-1

P. 126: Drawing, Study in Color and Form (USA), 2016; Thomas Gentille (American, b. 1936); Brush and watercolor, pen and ink on vellum; 38.7 × 31.1 × 4.4 cm (15 1/4 × 12 1/4 × 1 3/4 in.); 2017-26-1

PP. 130–131: Flurin with The Manhattan Piece. Photo: Miriam Künzli.

Unless otherwise stated, when three dimensions are listed, they are height x width x depth; when two are listed, they are height x diameter.

Acknowledgments

Curators' Acknowledgments

This book and the exhibition it accompanies, are the culmination of the support and assistance of many people both in and outside the museum.

First and foremost, the Cooper Hewitt curators wish to thank Susan Grant Lewin for her exceptional gift of contemporary jewelry. Getting to know Susan while working with her to select pieces for the museum was a delight, and a true education about the discerning collector's eye and the significance of contemporary jewelry.

Collaborating with consulting curator, Ursula Ilse-Neuman is always a pleasure. Her infectious passion for contemporary jewelry, expertise, and good humor were manifest throughout the project.

To the many jewelers who so willingly provided details about their work and shared their voices in these pages, we offer our deepest gratitude.

Many thanks to creative director Jiminie Ha and her team at With Projects, Jayson Payne, Fahad Al-Hunaif, and Jieun Yang who ensured that the book and exhibition design would be as striking as the jewelry in the Lewin Collection.

We thank Nancy Preu for her sensitive editing of the book's essay.

At Cooper Hewitt, we are especially grateful to Caroline Baumann, Director, whose enthusiasm and love of design has been an inspiration for this study of contemporary jewelry.

We thank Curatorial Director, Cara McCarty, whose leadership was critical in each phase of this acquisition, exhibition, and publication.

Special thanks must go to Masters Program Curatorial Fellows, Sebastian Grant and Susan Teichman. Their dedication and meticulous research and writing skills made them invaluable to the project from start to finish. Summer 2016 interns, Danielle Johnson and Kaitlin Macholz, played an important role in our early research and correspondence with so many jewelers.

Several Cooper Hewitt curators gave freely of their expertise and time to help with our queries and research: Emily Orr, Assistant Curator of Modern and Contemporary American Design, Caitlin Condell, Associate Curator of Drawings, Prints and Graphic Design, along with Caroline O'Connell and Julie Pastor also in that department.

This enlightening book and much of the digital content for the exhibition would not have been possible without the expert guidance of Pamela Horn, Director of Cross-Platform Publishing, assisted by Publications and Image Rights Associate, Matthew Kennedy, and intern Danielle Weindling.

We are delighted with the many beautiful images by photographer Matt Flynn and image technicians Alison Hale and Janice Hussain that grace these pages.

Additional thanks to the following museum staff: Conservators Annie Hall, Kira Eng-Wilmott, Perry Choe; Registrars Steve Langehough, Wendy Rogers, Kim Hawkins, Antonia Moser, and art handlers Larry Silver, Paul Goss; Jocelyn Groom, Yvonne Gomez-Durand, Matthew O'Connor, Mathew Weaver, and Maria Fernanda Alves da Silva of our exhibitions team; Mount maker, Jodi Hansen; Digital Production Associate, Chris Gauthier; Wendi Parson, Laurie Bohlk, Gregory Gestner, Alix Finkelstein in Communications and Marketing; Julie Barnes, Laura Meli, and Deborah Fitzgerald of Development; Susannah Brown in Education; Kathleen Kane and the Visitor Experience team.

Finally, we wish to recognize our families. To Cindy's husband, Roland, and son, Winston, and to Sarah's husband, Tom, deepest thanks for your patience and support.
—Cynthia Trope and Sarah D. Coffin,
Cooper Hewitt, Smithsonian Design Museum

Collector's Acknowledgments

Two people have been at my side since I began my collection: Thomas Gentille, one of America's greatest jewelers, who contributed greatly to the exhibition's installation, and Ursula Ilse-Neuman, who curated this exhibition, guided the book, and wrote an incredible essay.

For me, having two likeminded friends to discuss building the collection has added immeasurably to the experience. We had a lot of fun comparing notes, finding new jewelers, discussing who and which works were the strongest. It greatly added to the thrill of finding someone and something new and brilliant. I always treasure our times in Munich. Thank you both again for your complete dedication to the book and the show.

I am thankful for Caroline Baumann, the director of the Cooper Hewitt, who immediately responded to my collection with great enthusiasm and was so encouraging. Pamela Horn, Cara McCarty, Sarah Coffin, Cindy Trope, and the whole team at the museum have been incredibly helpful.

Thank you also to my family and friends who put up with my collecting. And a special thank you to all the jewelers whose work make up this fabulous collection. I am surrounded by jewels.
—Susan Grant Lewin

Author's Acknowledgments

This book and exhibition fulfill Susan Grant Lewin's long-standing pledge to share her collection with the general public, and it has been my delight to work with her and Cooper Hewitt to ensure that museum visitors will be able to enjoy her collection now and in the future.

My heartfelt thanks go, first and foremost, to Susan for her contagious passion and support of the field and ultimately for her confidence and trust in my expertise as she formed her collection over the preceding several decades. Jointly selecting the works to be donated to Cooper Hewitt brought back fond memories of our almost daily discussions and extensive travels to meet the artists and see the jewelry treasures that have now found their permanent home in the museum.
It has been a privilege to work with the museum's curatorial, editorial, and administrative staff. My special thanks to Cindy Trope, Associate Curator, who many years ago was my classmate at the Cooper Hewitt/Parsons Master's program, where we both learned to love the pleasures and challenges offered by the decorative arts and design. My deepest thanks also to Cooper Hewitt's Director, Caroline Baumann, as well as Cara McCarty, Curatorial Director, Pamela Horn, Director of Cross-Platform Publishing, and Curator Sarah Coffin, for the professionalism and insight they brought to the project, ensuring that the book and exhibition stayed true to everyone's goals and expectations.

Cooper Hewitt's talented curatorial fellows and interns, particularly Sebastian Grant and Susan Teichman, played a major role in the success of the exhibition and the publication through their verification of the countless facts and details that were vital to this ambitious undertaking.

Last but not least, I extend my deep gratitude and appreciation to all the artists whose creativity we celebrated here. Thank you for enriching our lives with your exceptional and thought-provoking works.
—Ursula Ilse-Neuman

Biographies

Painting by: Marc Seguin

Susan Grant Lewin

With over twenty years as a journalist, Susan Grant Lewin cut her design teeth as Design Editor of *Home Furnishings Daily* and then as Senior Editor of Design and Architecture at *House Beautiful Magazine*. A native Philadelphian, she is a graduate of the University of Pennsylvania.

Her close ties to the leaders of the architecture and design world enabled her to segue seamlessly into her position as Global Creative Director of Formica Corporation. Her strategy to reposition the seventy-five-year-old company was to commission new works utilizing the talents of the leading designers of the time. This was the beginning of using product demonstrations by designers to elevate a company's reputation. As part of her efforts, she worked with Frank Gehry, who created his groundbreaking ColorCore fish. A who's who of art and design, including Massimo and Lela Vignelli, Emilio Ambasz, Milton Glaser, Richard Artschwager, Haim Steinbach, and others, participated in the program. She curated several exhibitions including *Surface and Ornament*, which traveled globally, and *Material Evidence*, which originated at the Renwick Gallery of the Smithsonian American Art Museum. This is all documented in her Rizzoli book, *Formica & Design: From Counter Top to High Art* (1991).

Two of the winners of the *Surface and Ornament* competition were jewelers Bob Ebendorf and Ivy Ross. They charted the course of Lewin's interest in American jewelry. She commissioned artists to create jewelry for Formica, resulting in an exhibition. This deepened her interest in jewelry beyond Formica and led her to study the field. In 1994, she published a survey of American jewelry titled *One of a Kind: American Art Jewelry Today*.

After Formica, she founded her own public relations firm. Among her clients are some of the most talented designers and architects including James Dyson, Steven Holl, Charles Gwathmey, Michael Graves, and many others.

Ursula Ilse-Neuman

Ursula Ilse-Neuman is an independent curator, author, and lecturer specializing in contemporary art jewelry. She is Curator Emerita at the Museum of Arts and Design, New York, where, as curator from 1992 to 2014, she organized more than forty exhibitions in all media. Recent publications include "Unmistakably MacNeil" in *Linda MacNeil: Jewels of Glass* (2017), "Making Connections: the Jewelry of Richard Filipowski" in *Richard Filipowski* (Monograph 2017), *Multiple Exposures: Jewelry and Photography* (2014), *Light, Space, Structure: The Jewelry of Margaret De Patta* (2012), *Inspired Jewelry: Art Jewelry from the Collection* (2009), *Glass in Contemporary Jewelry* (2007), and *Zero Karats: The Donna Schneier Collection* (2006). She has been a juror for national and international exhibitions, including the Sonderschau Schmuck (Munich) and the International Jewelry Expo (Shanghai). She has lectured widely in the United States, Europe, and Asia. In 2011, she was invited to curate the American section of "Abhushan" in New Delhi, organized by the World Craft Council.